COUNCIL OF FASHION DESIGNERS OF AMERICA

AMERICAN FASHION COOKBOOK

© 2009 Assouline Publishing
601 West 26th Street, 18th Floor
New York, NY 10001, USA
Tel.: 212 989-6810 Fax: 212 647-0005
www.assouline.com
Color separation by Luc Alexis Chasleries
Printed in China
ISBN: 978 2 7594 0405 6

Cover Sketches: (Left) Roland Nivelais' Scallops Flambé
with Whiskey (recipe page 72);
Laura Poretzky's Simplest Sole Meuniere (recipe page 74).

COUNCIL OF FASHION DESIGNERS OF AMERICA

Foreword by Martha Stewart

AMERICAN
FASHION
COOKBOOK

Edited by Lisa Marsh

ASSOULINE

4

Foreword by Martha Stewart

Designers, by definition, are among the most creative people on earth. Inventiveness, cleverness, a great sense of proportion, a sensitivity to color and color combinations, and attention to structural details are inherent in their DNA. So it comes as no surprise that fashion people are also keenly interested in food, in its preparation, in its presentation, and in all kinds of recipes. I have eaten at several well-known designers' homes and I have always been greatly impressed with the kinds of foods they served.

Not long ago I was invited to attend a party at Videville, Valentino's grand chateau near Versailles. The grandeur and elegance of the house and the formality of the gardens were predictable—I had seen photographs of the place and read about its illustrious history and architecture. But nothing prepared me for the amazing feast that was served to the large group assembled for dinner on the outdoor terraces that summer evening. Golden brown bread boxes—covered rounds, squares, and rectangles—held delectable pastas of all kinds. Their thin, rigid crusts kept the food hotter than any fine porcelain would have. Mounds of sweet melon slices were stacked with alternating layers of hand-sliced proscuitto, emulating giant beehives. Salads were designed naturally but artistically, and all the ingredients were artfully combined, creating flavors that were intriguing and different. Platters of fresh buffalo mozzarella and tomatoes looked like works of art. The desserts, too, were simple but special—there was a memorable orange-almond olive oil torte and a ricotta cake that was especially sublime.

Dinner at Carolyne Roehm's country house was a gorgeous event, with a very long, blue-and-white bedecked table seating thirty or so guests on a wide loggia-like porch overlooking terraced parterre gardens. Despite the formality of the house, Carolyne favors simple, hearty, finger-licking food with farm-fresh ingredients, like barbecued ribs, corn pudding, biscuits, corn bread, and shortcakes and heavy cream—just the type of food we all love and crave.

The designers in this book, who have contributed recipes from their own personal collections, also surprise us. Zac Posen's butterscotch wafers are a must-have right away, as is Norma Kamali's olive oil popcorn. Elie Tahari's grilled lamb chops sound fabulous, and Michael Kors's pot roast divine. Many of these designers have appeared on my show, and now, in addition to showing their beautiful clothing, I can have them come cook these recipes. Ralph Rucci—please come and make your ricotta and spinach gnocchi?

Introduction

Fashion designers are masters of creating a mood, vibe, look and story with fabric, trimmings, thread, and accessories.

To many members of the Council of Fashion Designers of America, they create much more than clothing and accessories—they're creating components of the lifestyle brands they envision. Their visions extend to how they live, where they vacation, how they set a table, and yes, what they eat. This book is meant to build a bridge from clothing to the culinary world, while allowing you a glimpse inside these designers' lives and what inspires them.

And creating a recipe is not so far removed from creating a garment. "Cooking, to me, is exactly the same as designing a collection," admits Cynthia Rowley. "You have all these ingredients and you have to think of every detail."

While it may seem strange—funny even—that an industry that presents its wares on slender models has suggestions for what we should eat (or that we should eat at all), this is not the case. The fashion industry is full of Renaissance men and women, who advocate both fashion and food, as it works in their good lives.

For example, one of the most beloved members of the fashion industry, the late Bill Blass, was known for his simple meatloaf. He was a man who was true to his Indiana-born-and-bred palate, preferring good, basic food. He loved his meatloaf so, that when Lighthouse International awarded Blass with its Lifetime Achievement Award in 2000, Blass requested that his recipe be served as the main course at the gala. It was such a success, close friend Helen O'Hagan reports, that the room was full of cleaned plates.

Carolina Herrera is known for setting a wonderful table. Her recipe, for Pommes Toupinel —a twice-baked potato containing a poached egg—comes straight from her heart. She experienced love at first taste while having it as a twelve year old with her future sister-in-law and now, it's a multi-generational family favorite.

Behnaz Sarafpour has an insatiable sweet tooth. "When I go to a restaurant and look at the menu, I decide what dessert I'm going to have first before I pick out the rest of the meal," she says. Accordingly, baking sweets, like the strawberry shortcake she submitted for this book, is her non-fashion passion. She admits to specializing in gingerbread houses, Yule logs and intricately decorated baseball-themed cakes that she makes for her husband's birthday each year.

And Peter Som is such an accomplished foodie that he actually worked on creating a one-night-only restaurant several years ago for a benefit at Saks Fifth Avenue in Philadelphia. He is all about a higher class of comfort food, like the recipe he submitted for wonderfully complex minestrone.

Fashion designers also cook for their own. Jewelry designer Janis Savitt cooks healthy fare for her staff at lunchtime, while Zac Posen has been known to whip up dinner several times a month for his devoted employees.

Because America attracts designers from around the world, this collection includes recipes from such far-flung places as Armenia (Araks Yeramyan), Brazil (Francisco Costa), Chile (Sandra Muller), India (Naeem Khan), Malaysia (Yeohlee Teng), New Zealand (Rebecca Taylor), Scotland (Sue Stemp), and Turkey (Sylvia Heisel), among others.

And there is romance and sentiment worked into many of these dishes. John Varvatos first tried his Calaloo Soup while on vacation in Mustique with his then-girlfriend. They ate it again when they eloped there and now have a nanny from a neighboring island that brings them fresh calaloo (a Caribbean green leaf vegetable, also known as amaranth) from a special market in Brooklyn. Tommy Hilfiger enjoyed his mother's brownies most after school on cold, winter days in Elmira, NY. And Lela Rose's Brown Bread Ice Cream is a Southern classic, with her recipe being handed down for generations.

These recipes range from the most health conscious—Donna Karan's all-organic Green Juice—to the downright decadent—Keanan Duffty's Deep Fried Mars Bar. It is safe to say that most of them strike a balance somewhere between the two.

The idea of creating a book of fashion designers' recipes and sketches is not exactly a new one. The first compilation on this kind was assembled in 1990 for the first Seventh on Sale fundraiser for HIV and AIDs programs. A limited number of books were produced in a somewhat low-tech way (on a copy machine) and the book containing the original pieces of artwork was sold to the current CFDA president, Diane von Furstenberg. There are a number of gems in that book including a couple of "recipes" that instruct the readers how to "cook" a meal by ordering out.

American Fashion Cookbook is a slightly more serious recipe collection. As you can see, it's a long way from being assembled on a copy machine. Each one of these recipes is real and says something about the designer that has submitted it. Many of these illustrations are pieces of art you'd want to frame. We're thrilled to belong to an industry that is so creative on so many different levels and hope you enjoy many of these delicacies.

Bon appetit!

Steven Kolb
Executive Director
Council of Fashion Designers of America

Table of Contents

Chocolate Ganache by Rachel Roy
Recipe: Page 108

Eggs "Matt" ador
by Matt Murphy

INGREDIENTS

CHIPOTLE HOLLANDAISE SAUCE

- 3 egg yolks
- 1 tablespoon lemon juice
- 1 tablespoon water
- ½ teaspoon Sel Magique salt
- pinch of black pepper
- 2 sticks butter, melted
- 1 tablespoon Tabasco Chipotle pepper sauce

JALAPENO-CHEDDAR CORN CAKES

- 1 package Jiffy corn muffin mix
- 1 egg
- 1/3 cup milk

- 1 8-ounce can whole kernel corn, drained
- 1 jalapeno pepper, seeds removed, diced
- 1 small red pepper, diced
- 1 cup cheddar cheese, grated
- ½ teaspoon Sel Magique salt
- 6 slices nitrate-free ham OR 3 cups spinach
- 2 tablespoons olive oil
- 2-3 large cloves garlic, chopped

The trick to this recipe is timing. *Make* the sauce first and keep warm, then *make* the corn cakes, *then* the eggs, *combine* and serve. *Melt* butter in a small saucepan or in the microwave. Don't *overheat*; it should be warm, not hot. *Reserve.* In a separate stainless steel, enameled or glass saucepan, *beat* egg yolks with a wire whisk until slightly thickened. If you use an aluminum or iron saucepan, it will discolor the sauce. *Beat* in lemon juice, water, salt and pepper. *Place* saucepan over low heat and *stir* with the whisk until the egg mixture becomes smooth, creamy and thicker. *Remove* saucepan from heat. *Begin* adding melted butter a quarter teaspoon at a time, quickly beating in each addition before you add the next. When sauce is as thick as heavy cream, you may *beat* in butter by half tablespoons. It takes about 5 minutes to create the final emulsion. *Add* the hot sauce and stir. If the mixture is too thick, *add* a little hot water. To keep sauce warm, *set* saucepan in a larger pan of lukewarm water. To make the corn cakes, *preheat* oven to 400 degrees, *butter* a 13x18-inch cooking sheet. *Combine* muffin mix, egg and milk. *Fold* in corn, peppers and cheese. *Spoon* 8 individual portions of mixture onto baking sheet, about 3.5 inches in diameter, evenly spaced. *Bake* about at 400 degrees for 15 minutes. Don't *let* cakes brown—they will be too dry. *Remove* and cool on baking sheet. *Pan-brown* sliced ham. *Keep* warm. As an alternative to the meat, *sauté* spinach in olive oil with garlic. *Keep* warm. *Boil* water in a saucepan. *Put* eggs in saucepan gently, one-by-one, but no more than two or three at a time. The eggs cook in the boiled water, with the heat turned off, for exactly 3 minutes under cover. *Take* the eggs out with a slotted spoon. Each serving of Eggs "Matt"ador is two stacks of cakes and eggs. To *serve*, place 2 corn cakes onto a plate ringed with cilantro. *Place* ham (or spinach) on top of the cakes, then eggs. Generously *drizzle* the hollandaise sauce over each egg, and *garnish* with thin sliced lemon. *Dust* with paprika for color. *Serve.*

Banana Walnut Bread
by Mary Ping

INGREDIENTS

- 1 ½ cups flour
- ½ cup light brown sugar
- 2 teaspoons baking powder
- ½ teaspoon baking soda
- ½ teaspoon salt
- 2 eggs, beaten

- 1 ½ cups mashed ripe bananas (2-3 bananas)
- ¼ cup vegetable oil
- ¼ cup water
- ¾ cups granola (optional)
- 1 cup chopped walnuts

Preheat oven to 350 degrees. *Mix* flour, light brown sugar, baking powder, baking soda and salt in large bowl. *Beat* eggs in small bowl; stir in bananas, oil and water. *Add* egg mixture to flour mixture; *stir* just until moistened. *Stir* in granola and walnuts. *Pour* into greased 9x5-inch loaf pan. *Bake* at 350 degrees for 55 to 65 minutes or until toothpick inserted in center comes out clean. *Cool* 10 minutes; remove from pan. *Cool* completely on wire rack.

"Freshman year in college, I would bake banana bread as a break from all night paper writing sessions. It was a great way to use up the bananas, which were overripe and to fill the dorm kitchen with the best and most comforting aroma."

Sausage Puff
by Jeff Halmos, *Shipley Halmos*

INGREDIENTS
- *4 slices white bread, crusts removed*
- *1 pound mild pork sausage*
- *2 teaspoons prepared mustard*
- *1 cup Swiss cheese, grated*
- *4-5 scallions, chopped*
- *3 eggs*
- *2 cups half and half*

Place bread in a 9x13-inch baking dish. *Brown* and drain sausage. *Combine* with mustard and layer over bread. *Sprinkle* with the cheese and chopped scallions. Beat remaining ingredients together and pour mixture over casserole. *Refrigerate* overnight. *Bake* uncovered at 350 degrees for 45 minutes until the top begins to brown.

“My mom has been making this on Christmas morning for as long as I can remember. It's so simple to make. This is definitely a breakfast and, in our case, a holiday dish.”

Kuchen
by Monika Tilley

INGREDIENTS
- *1 stick butter*
- *⅞ cup sugar*
- *2 eggs*
- *1 teaspoon vanilla extract*
- *1 ¾ cups unbleached flour*
- *1 ½ teaspoons baking powder*
- *½ cup milk*
- *Seasonal fruit*
- *Dash of cinnamon*

“The toppings vary by season—blueberries, sliced apricots, peaches or apples.”

Preheat oven to 375 degrees. *Whip* butter, add sugar and eggs slowly and beat until fluffy. *Add* vanilla extract. Sift flour and baking powder. *Add* to butter mixture and then *mix* with milk until soft dough forms. *Pour* into a 9x12-inch baking dish, which has been greased and coated with plain bread crumbs. *Arrange* fruit on top, dust with sugar and a touch of cinnamon. *Bake* at 375 degrees for about 40 minutes. When cooled, *cut* into squares and serve.

The "Reutzler"
by Rachel Comey

INGREDIENTS
- *1 English muffin, toasted*
- *mayonnaise*
- *Canadian bacon, pan fried*
- *egg, fried*
- *sharp cheddar cheese, sliced*
- *fresh tomato, sliced*
- *salt and pepper*

"I acquired this recipe from the Warren Country Store in Warren, Vermont."

Spread mayonnaise on both halves of the English muffin. *Build* the sandwich from the bottom up, stacking Canadian bacon, egg, cheese, tomato, salt and pepper. *Enjoy.*

Alabama's Biscuits
by Natalie Chanin, *Alabama Chanin*

INGREDIENTS
- *1 stick cold, salted butter*
- *3 cups all-purpose flour*
- *2 teaspoons baking powder*
- *1 teaspoon salt*
- *¾ cup buttermilk*

Preheat oven to 425 degrees. *Sift* flour, baking powder and salt together in a large mixing bowl. *Cut* cold butter into flour using a pastry cutter. (Cold ingredients help to make biscuits fluffy.) *Add* buttermilk while stirring until mixture sticks together but is moist. *Turn* onto floured surface. *Knead* lightly until dough holds together. *Flatten* and roll with rolling pin to one half inch thick. *Fold* in half and roll again (always to approx. one half inch thick), repeating 6-8 times. Use a biscuit cutter to *cut* biscuits into rounds. *Bake* at 425 degrees for approximately 10 minutes or until golden brown. *Baste* with butter and serve.

"Before I started my collection, I spent a winter sabbatical on Los Roques, a small island off the coast of Venezuela. There I was allowed to help in the kitchen at Canto de Ballena, where I baked this simple southern bread. Word spread and my biscuits became famous on the island. Unable to pronounce the word 'biscuits,' they became known as "Pain de Alabama" and me, consequently as 'Alabama.' True story."

Croissant French Toast
by Edmundo Castillo

INGREDIENTS

- 4 croissants
- 1 egg
- 1 cup milk
- ½ teaspoon of vanilla
- ¼ teaspoon orange blossom extract
- fresh strawberries, sliced
- butter
- ground cinnamon
- maple syrup

Slice each croissant length-wise and *remove* some of the interior, creating a pocket. *Fill* with strawberries. In a bowl, *mix* the egg, milk, vanilla and orange blossom extract. Quickly *dip* the stuffed croissants in the egg mixture. *Be careful* not to get much mixture inside the croissants. *Melt* butter in a very hot skillet, *place* croissants in pan and reduce to medium. *Press* the croissants with a paddle and *allow* the strawberries to *cook* inside. When golden, *flip* the croissant. Once croissant is golden on both sides, *remove* from skillet, *sprinkle* with cinnamon and drizzle maple syrup. Blueberries, raspberries, bananas or peaches can be substituted for strawberries.

"Breakfast and brunch are my favorite meals. When I moved to Milan four years ago, one of the things I missed the most about New York was Sunday brunch. I started inviting friends over every Sunday and before I knew it, I was making different recipes every Sunday. During Milan fashion week, friends from New York would arrive straight from the airport and Croissant French Toast was one of the favorites. I served it with eggs, bacon, Kona coffee I hand carry back from Hawaii, and mimosas. I'm now back in New York but when I'm in Milan, the Sunday brunch tradition at my place is still going strong."

Blueberry Coffee Cake Muffins
by Carole Hochman

Taken from *The Barefoot Contessa* by Ina Garten

INGREDIENTS

- 12 tablespoons (1 ½ sticks) unsalted butter, room temperature
- 1 ½ cups sugar
- 3 extra-large eggs, room temperature
- 1 ½ teaspoons pure vanilla extract
- 8 ounces (about 1 cup) sour cream

- ¼ cup milk
- 2 ½ cups all-purpose flour
- 2 teaspoons baking powder
- ½ teaspoon baking soda
- ½ teaspoon kosher salt
- 2 half-pints fresh blueberries, picked through for stems

Preheat oven to 350 degrees. *Place* 16 paper liners in muffin pans. In the bowl of an electric mixer fitted with the paddle attachment, *cream* the butter and sugar until light and fluffy, about 5 minutes. With the mixer on low speed, *add* the eggs one at a time, *add* the vanilla, sour cream and milk. In a separate bowl, *sift* together the flour, baking powder, baking soda, and salt. With the mixer on low, *add* the flour mixture to the batter and *beat* until just mixed. *Fold* in the blueberries with a spatula until the batter is completely mixed. *Scoop* the batter into the prepared muffin pans, filling each cup just over the top, and *bake* at 350 degrees for 25 to 30 minutes, until the muffins are lightly browned on top and a caketester comes out clean.

Pip's Ultimate Kedgeree
by Nicholas Graham

INGREDIENTS

- 2 pounds cod or halibut
- 1 bay leaf
- parsely sprigs
- onion powder
- 2 cups water
- salt
- 1 tablespoon butter
- 2 ¼ cups Minute Rice

- ½ cup butter
- 1 small onion, chopped
- 8 hard boiled eggs, chopped
- 6 tablespoons parsley, chopped
- ⅔ cup cream
- 1 ½ tablespoons salt
- 2-3 tablespoons curry powder
- pepper

Put enough water in pan to cover fish, bay leaf, parsley and onion powder. *Bring* nearly to a boil, *put* in fish and *simmer* until barely cooked. *Drain*, skin, bone and flake fish, set aside. *Bring* two cups of water, salt and butter to a boil. *Add* Minute Rice and stir. When water comes to a boil, *remove* from heat and cover tightly. *After* at least 5 minutes, *fluff* rice with a fork. *Melt* ½ cup butter in large frying pan and fry onion until soft (not brown). *Add* curry powder and continue frying for two minutes or so. *Add* fish, eggs, parsley, cream, salt and pepper and *cook* for a few minutes. *Add* rice and stir thoroughly. If not serving immediately, *transfer* to casserole dish. *Reheat* in oven or microwave *stirring* occasionally.

Vidalia Onion Crustless Tart
by Victor Costa

INGREDIENTS

- *1 large Vidalia onion, coarsely chopped*
- *1 cup mayonnaise*
- *1 cup Swiss or Jarlsberg cheese, coarsly grated*
- *generous dashes of*
    Worcestershire sauce
    Tabasco sauce
    garlic powder
    dried thyme

Preheat oven to 350 degrees. *Combine* all ingredients gently in a large mixing bowl. *Spread* evenly in a 12-inch round fluted ceramic baking dish. *Bake* for 45 minutes or until tart is hot, brown and bubbling. For an authentic Southern touch, *spoon* onto Ritz crackers and serve.

Hot Artichoke and Spinach Spread
by Cindy Greene, *Libertine*

INGREDIENTS

- *8 ounces cream cheese*
- *1 cup mayonnaise*
- *1 package dry vegetable soup mix*
- *10 ounces frozen chopped spinach,*
    thawed and drained
- *14 ounces artichoke hearts (in water),*
    drained and chopped
- *3 cups mozzarella cheese, shredded*
- *Parmesan cheese*

Preheat oven to 350 degrees. *Mix* cream cheese, mayonnaise and dry soup mix in a large bowl. *Stir* in spinach, artichokes and mozzarella cheese. *Spread* mixture into a 2-quart baking dish and top with Parmesan cheese. *Bake* at 350 degrees for 30 minutes. *Serve* with crackers or Melba toast.

Yellowtail Crudo
by Derek Lam

INGREDIENTS
- *8-ounce piece of Yellowtail or Hamachi*
- *kosher salt*
- *½ bunch basil, cut into chiffonade for garnish*
- *¼ cup rice cracker balls*
        (available at Japanese specialty markets)

PICKLED WATERMELON
(make two days in advance)
- *1 ½ cups watermelon, diced*
- *1 cup water*
- *¾ cup white wine vinegar*
- *¼ cup sugar*
- *1 tablespoon salt*
- *½ jalapeno, with seeds intact*

MUSTARD CRÈME
- *¾ cup crème fraiche*
- *1 tablespoon Dijon mustard*
- *salt and pepper to taste*

❝This recipe for Hamachi crudo, presented by Chef Brendan McHale of Jack's Luxury Oyster Bar, is one of my all time favorites.❞

Yellowtail or hamachi is often confused with "Yellowfin" tuna. *Yellowtail* or Hamachi is a Japanese Amberjack. *Slice* fish into ¼-inch thick pieces with a very sharp, wet knife. When the knife has a thin slick of water on it, it will not stick to the meat and it will glide through the flesh easily. *Place* 4-5 bite size slices of yellowtail on each plate. *Season* fish with a pinch of kosher salt. *Place* one dice of watermelon on each piece of fish, then *place* equal sized dollop of mustard crème next to watermelon. *Sprinkle* with rice cracker balls, basil, and *drizzle* with extra virgin olive oil. *Serve* and *enjoy*.

PICKLED WATERMELON
Add everything but watermelon to a saucepan, *bring* to a boil, then simmer for 15 minutes. *Add* watermelon, simmer for 5 more minutes. *Cool* and refrigerate for 2 days, which is necessary for the watermelon to pickle.

MUSTARD CRÈME
Mix ingredients and *refrigerate*.

Cheese and Herb Bureks
by Sylvia Heisel

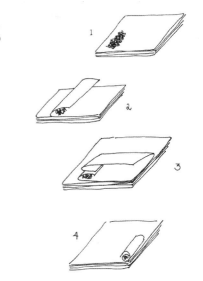

INGREDIENTS

- ½ small bunch Italian flat leaf parsley, leaves only, chopped
- ½ small bunch dill, fronds only, chopped
- 6 scallions, white ends only, chopped
- ½ pound feta cheese, crumbled
- 4 ounces cream cheese, softened
- 2 eggs, slightly beaten
- 1 pound phyllo dough, thawed
- ½ pound butter, melted

Preheat oven to 375 degrees. In a medium-sized bowl, *combine* filling ingredients. *Stir* with fork until well incorporated, *set* aside. *Cut* the stack of phyllo dough sheets lengthwise into two 12x8 inch rectangles. *Wrap* one rectangle in plastic wrap, *refrigerate* and reserve for future use. *Place* the other stack on a work surface, long side parallel to the edge of the counter. *Remove* one sheet of phyllo at a time and *cover* the remainder with a damp hand towel or paper towel to prevent drying. *Brush* the sheet lightly with melted butter. *Spread* about 1 tablespoon of filling in a strip three inches long and ½ inch wide toward the middle of the phyllo sheet, leaving 2 inches on the left side of the filling. (Illustration 1) *Fold* the 2-inch overlap over the filling. (Illustration 2) *Fold* the bottom of the sheet over the filling, *brush* with butter, then *fold* the top completely to enclose the filling. This will make a strip, with the enclosed filling on the left side. (Illustration 3) *Brush* the strip with butter. Starting at the filling end, *gently* roll the strip into a cylindrical borek about 3 inches long and 1 inch wide. (Illustration 4) *Place* borek on buttered baking sheet, seam side down with other phyllo sheets, spacing boreks slightly apart on baking sheet. *Brush* with melted butter. *Bake* for 30-35 minutes until golden brown. To make in advance, *prepare* boreks and freeze on a baking sheet. When they're frozen, *remove* from baking sheet and store in an air-tight container or bag. *Thaw* on baking sheet in the refrigerator, then *bake* as directed.

> **❝My mother was raised in Istanbul and the little bit of cooking I do is from her recipes. These appetizers are the samosas of the Middle East and are almost as common in Turkey as baklava.❞**

Goat Cheese Tarts with Arugula Salad
by Andreas Melbostad, *PHI*

INGREDIENTS
- *prepared puff pastry (frozen from Dufour Pastry Kitchen)*
- *goat cheese*
- *fresh thyme*
- *red onion, chopped*
- *honey*
- *salt and pepper*
- *arugula*
- *olive oil*
- *honey*
- *Dijon mustard*
- *lemon*
- *salt and pepper*

Pre-heat oven to 390 degrees. *Roll* out pastry on a lightly floured surface until 1/8 inch thick. *Cut* into 4x4-inch squares. *Place* the following in the center of each square: red onion, thyme, one generous tablespoon goat cheese, a generous teaspoon honey and freshly ground salt and pepper. *Bring* the four corners of the pastry together covering the filling. *Bake* for 20-30 minutes until golden. *Mix* equal parts olive oil, honey, Dijon mustard and lemon to make honey mustard vinaigrette. *Drizzle* over arugula, add salt and pepper and *serve* with warm goat cheese tarts.

" My goat cheese/arugula salad appetizer brings back memories from my time in Paris. It is a French brasserie staple. I enjoy preparing this as an appetizer for friends. It also works well made into small hors d'oeuvres without the salad. "

"Crowd Pleaser" Cocktail Spread

by Steven Stolman

INGREDIENTS

- *1 package finely shredded cheddar cheese*
- *1 package REAL bacon bits (always near the salad dressings in the supermarket)*
- *1 bunch of scallions*
- *Hellmann's Mayonnaise*
- *Worcestershire Sauce*
- *fresh ground black pepper*
- *Ritz Crackers (the best) or Melba toast rounds (getting harder to find)*

In a food processor fitted with the metal blade, *finely* chop scallions and bacon bits until they look almost predigested. *Add* cheese and pulse the food processor until combined. *Add* a few dashes of Worcestershire sauce and then enough mayonnaise to create a smooth but tight spread. It shouldn't look like cheese, or bacon, or anything else recognizable, which is part of the charm of this thing. *Season* with black pepper and pile into a chic bowl (I like a small silver Revere bowl). *Surround* with crackers and a nice little spreader. *Make* yourself a cocktail and pretend you're Lovey and Thurston Howell. I promise there will be no leftovers. I have even seen guests lick the bowl clean. Honestly.

"I am embarrassed to admit that I'm a serial entertainer. Even when I was just a young Seventh Avenue worker bee, my little apartment always seemed to be the gathering place for all my buddies for after work drinks, a tradition that I still truly enjoy, no matter where I am living or what I am doing. This easy to make ahead, and is a rather retro concoction—one of those crazy things that people actually make special requests for when they know they are coming over to my place. It's my pleasure to share."

Le Panier de Crudites
by Catherine Malandrino

INGREDIENTS

- *1 artichoke*
- *carrots*
- *celery stalks*
- *3 tomatoes*
- *radishes*
- *cauliflower*
- *red pepper*
- *green pepper*
- *2 eggs, hard boiled*
- *1 teaspoon olive oil*

L'ANCHOIADE PROVENCAL

- *5 teaspoons anchovy cream*
- *½ clove garlic, minced*
- *3 tablespoons extra virgin olive oil*

ANCHOVY CREAM

- *4 flat anchovy fillets*
- *2 large garlic cloves, minced*
- *1 ¼ cups heavy cream*

Make anchovy cream by mixing ingredients together until smooth. To prepare L'Anchoiade Provencale, *mix* garlic and anchovy cream. *Add* in the olive oil, little by little. *Arrange* the vegetables and the eggs in a straw or wicker basket. *Pour* the Anchoiade into a ramekin and place it in the basket to present your hors d'oeuvre.

"Serve on a white tablecloth along with un Rosé de Provence, the song of the cicadas as music and a field of lavender as a landscape.**"**

Cheese Börek
by Araks Yeramyan

INGREDIENTS

- *4 eggs*
- *½ cup olive oil*
- *2 cups milk*
- *8 ounces sharp cheddar cheese, shredded*
- *8 ounces cottage cheese*
- *8 ounces feta cheese, crumbled*
- *1 package phyllo dough*

Preheat oven to 350 degrees. In a large bowl, *beat* eggs and *combine* olive oil and milk. *Add* cheddar, cottage and feta cheeses. In a 10x14-inch baking dish, layer two sheets of phyllo dough. *Pour* a ladle of cheese mixture on top of the phyllo, distributing evenly. *Add* two more sheets of phyllo, each one covering half of the dish, making sure that the phyllo is rippled. *Repeat* until there are two sheets of phyllo remaining. *Make* sure the cheese mixture is evenly distributed throughout the dish. There should be no phyllo sections untouched by cheese. *Lay* the final two sheets and *cover* with the remaining cheese mixture. The top layer should have more cheese mixture than the rest of the pastry. *Bake* for one hour. The borek is done when the top is golden brown. *Allow* to sit at room temperature for 10 to 15 minutes before serving.

Stuffed Bacon Wrapped Dates
by Selima Salaun, *Selima Optique* and *Bond 07*

INGREDIENTS
- *24 large dates, pitted*
- *12 slices bacon, cut in half (24 pieces)*
- *4 ounces goat cheese*
- *24 unsalted almonds, toasted*

Preheat oven to 500 degrees. Stuff each date with an almond, then *fill* the remaining space with softened goat cheese using a pastry bag. *Wrap* a piece of bacon around each date and *secure* with a toothpick. *Place* dates on baking sheet lined with parchment paper and bake 6 to 8 minutes on top oven rack until bacon is golden and crispy. Cool briefly before serving.

❝I like this dish because it is sweet and salty at the same time, easy to make and all my guests love it. If they do not eat meat, you can prepare a few stuffed dates without the bacon and it still tastes delicious. I make it for intimate dinners and serve it with a nice glass of champagne or wine. You can check with my friend Catherine Malandrino—she loves it!❞

Andalusian Gazpacho
by Tory Burch

INGREDIENTS

- 6 large ripe tomatoes (about 2 pounds)
- 1 large cucumber, peeled, seeded, diced (about 1 ½ cups)
- 1 green bell pepper, chopped
- 1 red onion, chopped
- 1 cup tomato juice
- ½ cup bottled clam juice

- 3 tablespoons red wine vinegar
- 2 tablespoons olive oil
- 2 tablespoons fresh lemon juice
- 2 tablespoons fresh basil, chopped
- 2 tablespoons fresh parsley, chopped
- 2 ½ teaspoons Old Bay seasoning
- 8 ounces cooked shrimp, cut into 1/2- inch pieces

Blanch tomatoes in large pot of boiling water 30 seconds. *Drain*. *Refresh* under cold running water. *Peel* tomatoes. *Halve* tomatoes crosswise. Working over small bowl, *squeeze* gently to extract seeds. *Discard* seeds. *Transfer* tomatoes to food processor. *Blend* until coarsely pureed. *Transfer* tomatoes to large bowl. *Stir* in all remaining ingredients. *Season* gazpacho to taste with salt and pepper. *Chill* until cold, about 2 hours. This gazpacho can be made 1 day ahead. *Cover* and keep refrigerated. *Serve* cold.

"This recipe has been in my family for years. You can make it the night before (it tastes even better when the flavors have blended overnight) and serve it with a big salad and sliced baguette for an easy summer lunch. I serve this at our beach house when we have our friends and family over and even my three little boys love it. It's a great way to get children to eat their vegetables!"

Cucumber Soup
by Stan Herman

INGREDIENTS

- 6 to 8 medium cucumbers, peeled, seeded, cut into chunks
- 2 medium yellow onions, chopped into chunks
- 1 leek, sliced up to the dark green
- 2 celery stalks, sliced including leaves at the end
- 3 tablespoons butter
- 2 generous dabs olive oil
- a healthy pinch thyme
- salt and pepper to taste
- 1 quart chicken or vegetable stock (or there is always water from the tap)
- juice of 1 lemon

Sautee the cucumbers, onions, and celery for 5 minutes in butter and oil. *Pour* in stock. *Add* thyme, salt and pepper to taste. *Let* simmer until vegetables are very soft, and then let cool. *Pour* ingredients into the blender with lemon juice. *Blend* until it becomes pale green. *Let* it rest and then adjust the taste by adding more lemon, salt, or pepper. *Serve* cool with a slice of lemon floating on the velvety broth. It goes great with a crust of bread and my favorite white wine, Pouilly Fumé. I promise it will hook you and your company with its seductive personality.

"What is better than a bowl of soup to bring a group of friends together? In fact, during late fall and through the gray of winter there is usually a stock pot purring on my stove. Almost every soup starts with a vegetable mirepox; carrots, celery and a leek or onion. It becomes a good base for leftover meats and poultry—never vegetables since they have to be added fresh to retain their best flavor. But this recipe is for the sunniest soup of summer, best served chilled, for it is in summer that most of my friends crowd around the butcher block."

Indian Lentil Soup
by Naeem Khan

INGREDIENTS

- *¼ cup yellow dal (Moong dal)*
- *¼ cup red dal (puy lentils)*
- *¼ cup channa dal (Horse gram)*
- *¼ cup beluga dal*
- *¼ cup cracked wheat*
- *¼ cup pink dal (Mansoor dal)*
- *¼ cup quinoa*
- *5 cups water*
- *½ cup extra virgin olive oil*
- *½ stick salted butter, melted*
- *1 medium red onion, chopped small*
- *4 large acorn squash*
- *2 medium tomatoes, diced*
- *4 cloves garlic, sliced*
- *1 Serrano chili, chopped*
- *juice of 1 lime*
- *ginger, a 4-inch piece, skinned and sliced*
- *cilantro leaves*
- *10 curry leaves*
- *¼ tsp cumin*
- *¼ tsp mustard seed*
- *1 tsp sea salt*
- *½ tsp curry powder*
- *1 teaspoon low-fat yogurt*

Wash lentils (dal) and grains. In a large, heavy pot, *boil* lentils and grains with 5 cups of water, tomatoes, ginger and salt for about 45 minutes. *Add* water if needed. *After* mixture is cooked, remove the ginger pieces and discard. In a medium pot, *heat* ½ cup virgin olive oil. *Add* cumin, mustard seeds and chopped onion. *Sauté* until golden. *Add* curry leaves, garlic and Serrano chili, *cook* for two minutes, *lower* the heat. *Add* curry powder and cook for another minute. *Add* this mixture to the lentil mixture and stir well. *Cut* the top 2 inches of the squash to form a cup. *Scoop* out the seeds and fiber, and cut the small tip from the bottom, so the squash will sit flat in a soup bowl. *Rub* butter on the inside and the outside of the squash. *Heat* oven to 375 degrees and bake for about 45 minutes. To *serve*, put squash "cups" in soup bowls; *pour* lentils into acorn. *Add* ½ teaspoon lime juice, rock salt to taste, yogurt and garnish with cilantro leaves. *Make* sure to scoop the squash with each bite of lentils.

> " This soup was cooked in my mother's north Indian country home in a clay pot on a slow wood fire. It's a great fall and winter dish. Lentils make a wholesome, healthy meal. "

Coconut Fish Chowder
by Sigrid Olson

INGREDIENTS

- 2 pounds halibut or cod fillet
- 2 cans coconut milk
- 1 pint chicken broth
- 1 knob fresh ginger, peeled and chopped finely (about ¼ cup)
- 2 cloves garlic, minced
- 1 cup cooked jasmine rice
- 3 tablespoons chopped fresh cilantro
- ½ cup fresh corn kernels (cut off the cob if possible)
- ½ cup freshly squeezed lime juice
- olive oil
- sea salt (or kosher salt) to taste

Coat the bottom of a large soup pot with olive oil and sauté garlic and ginger for a couple of minutes over medium heat. *Cut* fish fillets into large chunks and add to pot. *Stir* to mix fish and garlic/ginger well. *Add* coconut milk and chicken broth. *Simmer* mixture over a low heat for about 15 minutes until the fish flakes apart. *Add* corn and cooked jasmine rice and stir. *Simmer* a few more minutes. *Add* lime juice and fresh cilantro just before serving.

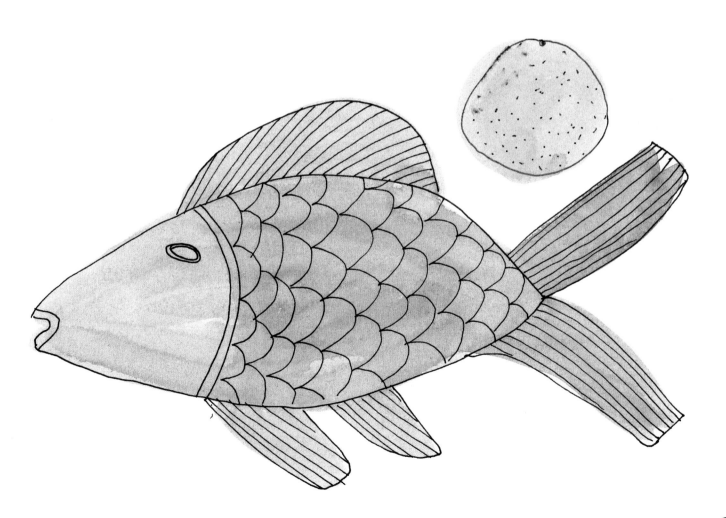

Tortilla Soup
by Nicole Miller

INGREDIENTS

- *1 tablespoon canola oil*
- *1 medium onion, chopped*
- *1 clove garlic, finely chopped*
- *2 medium jalapeno chiles, seeded and chopped*
- *4 roasted tomatoes, peeled, seeded, and chopped*
- *4 cups chicken broth*
- *1 can white hominy drained*
- *1 ½ cups chicken, shredded*
- *corn tortillas*
- *½ teaspoon salt*
- *½ teaspoon cumin*
- *¼ cup canola oil*
- *1 medium avocado*
- *½ cup shredded Monterey jack cheese*
- *fresh cilantro, chopped*
- *1 lime, cut into wedges*

Heat oil and add onions. *Cook* 2 minutes, stirring frequently. *Add* garlic and jalapeños and *cook* for a few minutes. *Add* chopped tomatoes and chicken broth. *Bring* to a boil, then *add* hominy and simmer for 20 minutes. *Add* shredded chicken. *Season* with salt and cumin. *Cut* tortillas into thin stips ¼ inch or less with sharp knife or scissors. *Fry* strips in oil until crisp. To *serve*, *peel* and *pit* avocado and *cut* into 1-inch slices. *Divide* half of the tortillas strips among serving bowls. *Add* soup. *Top* with avocado and cheese. *Garnish* with remaining tortilla strips and cilantro. *Serve* with lime wedges.

My Minestrone
by Peter Som

INGREDIENTS

- ½ pound pancetta, cubed
- extra virgin olive oil
- 6 garlic cloves, sliced
- 1 large yellow onion, large dice
- 3-4 celery stalks, medium dice
- 3 carrots, large dice
- 2 tablespoon rosemary, minced
- kosher salt
- black pepper
- 1 14-ounce can cannellini beans, drained and rinsed
- 1 large can San Marzano whole tomatoes
- 2 cups diced zucchini
- 2 cups yellow/summer squash
- 1 large russet potato, diced
- 8 cups homemade chicken stock (It makes a difference, but store bought is fine too.)
- ¼ to ½ teaspoon chili pepper flakes
- 1 bay leaf
- 1 or 2 rinds Parmesano-Reggiano
- 1 bunch kale, chopped
- Flat-leaf parsley, roughly chopped

Sauté pancetta with olive oil in a large pot over medium heat until slightly brown around edges then *add* garlic and sauté for another minute. *Add* onion, celery, carrot, rosemary, some salt and pepper and sauté approx 10 min or until veg is tender. *Add* beans, tomatoes, zucchini, summer squash and potato. *Add* Salt and pepper. *Add* chicken stock, chili pepper flake, bay leaf and parmesan rind. *Simmer* 15 or so minutes, or until vegetables are tender. *Skim* foam off the top. Ideally here is where you fish out the bay leaf. Or just warn your guests not to eat it if they find it. *Add* the kale and continue to simmer until wilted–approx 2-3 minutes. *Toss* in the parsley. *Serve* with a hunk of Parmesano- Reggiano and a microplane—to be grated at the table. If you want to add chicken—*drizzle* some chicken breast with salt, pepper and olive oil, *roast* on a sheet pan at 450 for 20 minutes, or until done. *Cube* and add to each bowl. If you want to fancy up the soup, *omit* the kale and *add* 2 cups sautéed wild mushrooms (such as cremini) as well as ¼ to ½ a cup of heavy cream at the very end.

66 I've cobbled together various recipes—including my mom's and my sister's—to get my minestrone right. There isn't any way you can mess this up and the variations are endless. I don't add pasta to mine, but if you want to go traditional, go ahead and add any small shaped pasta such as gemelli or farfalle. This soup is even better the next day. 99

Roasted Cauliflower Soup
by Cathy Waterman

INGREDIENTS

- *2 large heads cauliflower*
- *3 cloves garlic*
- *olive oil*
- *coarse sea salt*
- *2 large red or yellow onions, thinly sliced in rounds*
- *1 hot red pepper, as hot as you'd like*
- *1 sweet red pepper, sliced*
- *3 cups cooked chick peas (I prefer to prepare them myself, but will use canned when I don't have the time to soak and cook them.)*
- *sea salt*
- *fresh thyme*
- *vegetarian broth cubes*
- *1 medium bunch black kale*
- *whole grain bread*
- *garlic olive oil*

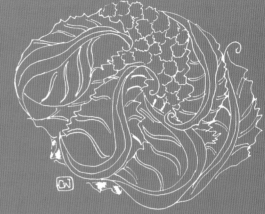

Cut the stems from the black kale and lightly steam. When cool, *slice* thinly. For garlic croutons, *brush* good whole grain bread with garlic olive oil, *cut* into chunks and bake at 350 degrees until lightly browned. *Clean* cauliflower and break into small florettes. *Place* in a pan with garlic cloves and coat lightly with oil and salt. *Roast* the cauliflower at 350 degrees, checking on the mixture every 20 minutes or so, mixing it so that it roasts evenly. When it's done, it looks moist, is a caramel color and tastes sweet. *Make* a broth by adding three cups of water to a large soup pot with two broth cubes. *Bring* to a boil. In a sauté pan, heat oil and add onions, thyme and some salt. *Cook* on medium until the onions start to brown. *Add* hot and sweet peppers and the cooked chick peas. *Place* the cauliflower and the chick pea mixture into a blender or a food processor and blend until really smooth. *Transfer* to a soup pot and *thin* with broth until it can be easily ladled into soup bowls. *Season* with salt and pepper. *Heat* and serve on a bed of kale, sprinkled with croutons.

❝ My family could go days eating just this soup. Cavolo Nero (black kale) has become easy to find in the last few years. It's deep, dark green and also called 'Italian kale.' This last year, Russian and peacock kale have appeared and are a great substitute. ❞

Calaloo Soup
by John Varvatos

INGREDIENTS
- *1 bunch calaloo*
- *1 cup chicken broth*
- *1 small onion, chopped*
- *2 cloves of garlic, chopped*
- *Salt and pepper to taste*
- *Chili powder, if you like it spicy*

Wash and chop calaloo leaves. *Add* calaloo, onion and garlic to a pot with 1 cup of water. *Bring* to a boil and cook until calaloo is soft, about 10 minutes. *Remove* from heat and cool. *Blend* until smooth in blender or food processor. *Put* mixture back in pot with chicken broth and *simmer* for another 10 minutes. Salt and pepper to taste.

Cullen Skink (Traditional Scottish Fish Soup)
by Sue Stemp

INGREDIENTS
- *5 cups milk*
- *2 pounds smoked haddock*
- *½ cup butter*
- *2 large onions, diced*
- *2 tablespoons all–purpose flour (Alternatively, you could substitute 1 pound of potatoes, peeled, cut-up and cooked.)*
- *1 ¼ cups heavy cream*
- *fresh squeezed lemon juice*
- *salt and freshly ground black pepper*
- *2 tablespoons parsley, finely chopped*
- *Carrots, zucchini and turnips cut in julienne strips (optional)*

Pour milk into a large saucepan and *bring* to a boil. *Remove* from heat and add haddock. Let stand for 10 minutes. *Melt* butter in a saucepan and gently fry the onions for 10 minutes, until soft but not browned. *Stir* in flour and cook for 5 minutes. *Gradually* add the haddock milk, stirring all the time until the soup is smooth and slightly thickened. *Add* the haddock and simmer over a low heat for 10 minutes. *Transfer* the soup to a food processor or blender and blend for a few seconds until smooth. *Pass* through a fine sieve or a strainer into a clean saucepan and stir in the cream. *Reheat* to just below boiling point. *Season* to taste with lemon juice, salt and pepper. *Ladle* into warm bowls, garnished with thin strips of carrot, zucchini, turnip and chopped parsley. *Serve* with hot crusty bread and butter.

Gardener's Pasta Salad
by Dianne Benson

INGREDIENTS

- 1 pound fresh pasta
- 2 Belgian endives, cut into ½-inch pieces
- 1 fennel bulb, sliced into long strips (don't use stalks)
- 4 scallions, chopped, both green and white parts
- 1 clove garlic, minced (elephant or golden garlic preferred)
- 6-8 baby artichoke hearts, halved (canned will do)
- 4-6 pitted black olives, thinly sliced
- 1 pint red or yellow cherry tomatoes, halved
- 1 bunch watercress, chopped
- 1 cup baby salad leaves or baby arugula
- basil leaves, shredded
- tender fresh thyme leaves, stems removed
- salt and ground black pepper
- pine nuts or pistachio nuts
- ½ cup Parmesan cheese, freshly grated
- ¼ cup virgin olive oil (the greener the better)
- juice of 1 lemon

There is nothing to this but the assemblage of the ingredients, so *have* them all lined up before the pasta water comes to a full boil. *Cook* the pasta until the desired degree of doneness. *Drain* well and put into a large and beautiful bowl, preferably something footed, floral and hand-painted. *Combine* all the ingredients into the bowl and toss thoroughly. *Top* with whatever flower is freshest in the garden for the lovely look. (Violets, pansies or nasturtiums are always charming.)

"You don't need to grow the ingredients yourself, but the fresher the better. This can be served warm, but it's better at room-temperature.**"**

Raw Corn Salad
by Rod Keenan

INGREDIENTS

- *corn kernels from 4 raw corn cobs*
- *½ cup celery, chopped*
- *½ cup pomegranate seeds*
- *½ cup parsley, chopped*
- *¼ cup fresh lime juice*
- *¼ cup olive oil*
- *coarse sea salt and ground pepper to taste*
- *1 tablespoon Rus al Hanout*

RUS AL HANOUT

- *1 tablespoon fennel seeds*
- *1 tablespoon coriander seeds*
- *1 tablespoon black mustard seeds*
- *1 tablespoon cumin seeds*
- *1 cinnamon stick grated*
- *3 star anise*
- *5 dried bay leaves*
- *1 teaspoon ground cloves*
- *1 teaspoon ginger*
- *1 teaspoon allspice*
- *1 teaspoon cayenne*
- *1 really generous pinch of saffron*
- *2 tablespoons dried rose petals*

In a large bowl, *toss* together corn, celery, pomegranate and parsley. In a jar with a lid, *mix* the olive oil, lime juice, salt, pepper and rus al hanout. Seal and shake well. *Pour* the oil mixture over the corn mixture, and gently *stir* to coat all ingredients. *Cover* and chill at least 3 hours in the refrigerator before serving.

RUS AL HANOUT

Combine above ingredients with a mortar and pestle.

"CORN - UCOPIA"

"CORN" SILK THREAD

AFRICAN TRADE BEADS GLASS VINTAGE

FRENCH GROSGRAIN BINDING

Joe's Caesar Salad
by Henry Jacobson

INGREDIENTS

- *2 romaine lettuce hearts*
- *4 ounces Parmesan cheese, grated*
- *2 large garlic cloves, finely chopped*
- *1 tablespoon anchovies, finely chopped*
- *1 tablespoon fresh lemon juice*
- *1 teaspoon powered mustard*
- *3 tablespoons extra virgin olive oil*
- *1 tablespoon red wine vinegar*
- *1 tablespoon Worcestershire sauce*
- *1 splash Tabasco sauce*
- *¼ teaspoon freshly ground black pepper*
- *1 raw egg*

CROUTONS
- *1 loaf French bread*
- *extra virgin olive oil*
- *garlic salt*

Wash, *dry*, and *chop* lettuce leaves and place in large bowl. *Toss* with 3 ounces grated Parmesan cheese. In a small bowl, *mix* chopped garlic, anchovies, lemon juice, powered mustard, olive oil, red wine vinegar, Worcestershire sauce, Tabasco sauce and pepper. *Add* raw egg and whisk thoroughly to create dressing. *Pour* dressing over lettuce and *sprinkle* with remaining Parmesan cheese. *Add* pepper to taste. *Top* with croutons (see below).

CROUTONS

Slice bread into small crouton size squares. *Sauté* in olive oil until slightly browned. *Season* with garlic salt to taste. Croutons should remain uncovered after cooking to harden.

" This recipe was obtained through years of rapt observation of the talented wait staff at a favorite local restaurant, not surprisingly called Joe's. I have tweaked a few ingredients over the years based on personal taste, but the recipe remains faithful to the original. "

Humilitas con Ensalata Chilena
by Sandra Muller

INGREDIENTS

CORN MIXTURE
- *3 ½ cups fresh white corn kernels and corn husks*
- *½ cup milk*
- *salt and freshly ground black pepper*
- *1 onion, chopped*
- *1 tablespoon fresh cilantro, chopped*

TOMATO SALAD
- *4 cups onions, finely chopped*
- *4 cups tomatoes, peeled and sliced.*

- *salt and pepper*
- *3 tablespoons olive oil*
- *coriander and basil, chopped*

PISCO SOUR
- *1 ½ ounces Pisco*
- *½ ounce fresh lemon juice*
- *1 teaspoon sugar*
- *½ egg white*

Puree the corn kernels with milk in food processor. *Add* salt and pepper to taste. In a large frying pan, *heat* some olive oil, and *saute* the onion and cilantro for 10 minutes. *Add* pureed corn and cook, *stirring* continuously until it thickens. One at a time, *remove* each husk and *spread* about 4 tablespoons of the corn mixture in the center of each husk. *Fold* the husk around the corn mixture to make a square packet, and *tie* securely with kitchen string. *Make sure* that all the edges are sealed, and that no batter can escape from the husk. When all of the husks are filled, *place* them in a large pot of salted water to cover, *simmer* on low heat, covered, for about 1 hour. *Serve* in the husks, warm with tomato salad and Pisco Sour.

FOR THE TOMATO SALAD
Rinse onions thoroughly in cold water. *Drain* in bowl, *mix* tomatoes with onions. *Season* to taste with salt and pepper. *Add* olive oil and mix well. *Sprinkle* with chopped coriander and basil. *Serve*. Shake in iced cocktail shaker and strain.

FOR THE PISCO SOUR
Shake in iced cocktail shaker and strain.

66 My friends always expect Chilean dishes when they come to my house. Many have enjoyed this dish including Goldie Hawn and Aamir Khan when visiting Los Angeles for his Oscar nomination of Bollywood movie *Lagaan*. 99

Mom's Chinese Chicken Salad
by Blake Kuwahara, *Base Curve Eyewear*

INGREDIENTS
- ½ pound cooked chicken breasts
- 2 ounces Mei Fun (Chinese rice sticks)

SALAD
- 1 head Iceberg lettuce, shredded
- 4 stalks green onion, chopped
- 2 tablespoon toasted sesame seeds
- Chinese parsley (cilantro) chopped

DRESSING
- 1 teaspoon Accent
- 2 tablespoons salt
- ½ teaspoon cracked pepper
- ¼ cup vegetable oil
- 1 tablespoon sesame oil
- 3 tablespoons vinegar

Make salad dressing (see below). *Boil* chicken in small amount of water with salt, carrots, celery and onions. *Discard* vegetables and shred chicken after boiling. *Deep fry* rice sticks in hot oil. *Toss* salad ingredients, *add* dressing and *serve*.

FOR THE DRESSING
Combine dressing ingredients and *blend* well. *Chill*.

"Although I'm a fourth-generation Japanese-American, this Chinese Chicken Salad has been part of our special family gatherings (Christmas, Thanksgiving, Easter, baby showers, birthdays—you name it!) as long as I can remember. No matter what's being served, this salad somehow complements the menu. And, just so that it's solidified in our collective family memories, it's also been served in the same large, smoked brown-grey salad bowl from the '70s (which now looks very 'of-the-moment')."

Tuscan Summer Salad
by Holly Dunlap

INGREDIENTS

- 3 cups organic cherry tomatoes
- 1 cup organic canned corn
- 1 cup aged pecorino cheese, diced
- 2 organic asparagus bundles (if asparagus is not in season, use string beans)
- ½ cup fresh pesto (fresh basil leaves, grated Parmigiano-Reggiano cheese, pine nuts, minced garlic, extra-virgin olive oil mixed in a blender)
- chopped grilled shrimp or chicken (optional)

Chop asparagus into bite-sized pieces and *steam* on low, being careful to leave a bit of crunch. *Cut* cherry tomatoes into quarters and *put* into a big bowl. *Add* corn, diced cheese, steamed asparagus. *Stir* in pesto. *Season* with salt, pepper or olive oil as needed. *Add* chopped grilled shrimp or chicken if desired. *Eat* immediately or *chill* (keeps well in refrigerator for 2-3 days).

> "Tuscan Summer Salad can also be used as sauce on angel hair pasta by adding extra-virgin olive oil. If salad begins to wilt a bit over time, use leftovers to make a delicious egg soufflé or quiche."

Cesarani Summer Pasta
by Sal Cesarani

INGREDIENTS

- *2 cloves of garlic, chopped*
- *6 large ripe tomatoes, chopped*
- *fresh basil, chopped*
- *1 cup extra virgin olive oil*
- *salt and pepper to taste*
- *1 pound of penne or rigatoni*
- *1 wedge of good Brie*

In a big bowl, *mix* the chopped tomatoes, garlic, and basil. *Pour* olive oil over the ingredients, salt and pepper to taste. *Cover* with plastic and put into the sun to warm, until pasta is ready to serve. *Cut* cheese into cubes and place into sun-warmed tomato mix. *Boil* water for pasta to cook until al dente. *Drain* pasta. Pour into tomato and cheese mixture and toss. *Serve* immediately. Best accompanied with a fresh green salad, warm bread, and a good glass of wine.

Henry's Basil Chicken with Linguine
by Henry Grethel

INGREDIENTS

- *4 skinless, boneless chicken breasts*
- *1 teaspoon salt*
- *¾ teaspoon pepper*
- *¼ cup flour (for dusting)*
- *¼ cup extra virgin olive oil*

- *½ cup dry vermouth or dry white wine*
- *1 cup heavy cream (to cover chicken cutlets)*
- *soy sauce (to taste)*
- *fresh basil*
- *linguine*

Pound chicken breasts. *Season* with salt and freshly ground pepper. *Dust* lightly with flour. *Sauté* cutlets in olive oil. *Add* wine and lower heat to a simmer. *Slowly* add heavy cream. *Add* soy sauce (to taste). Add fresh chopped basil. *Garnish* with fresh basil sprigs and serve with linguine.

Tagliatelle Barbequenese
by Alexander Julian

INGREDIENTS
- 2 ½ cups of Barbequenese Sauce
- 1 ½ pounds tagliatelle (DeChecco is my personal favorite)
- 1 ½ tablespoons of salt
- ½ cup freshly grated Parmesan cheese
- 6 bottles of Kunde Zinfandel

BARBEQUENESE SAUCE
- ¾ pounds Carolina barbeque (pork ribs)
- 1/3 cup Zinfandel
- 2 cups Italian tomatoes, roughly chopped
- 3 tablespoons each of celery and carrots, chopped
- 3 tablespoons freshly squeezed garlic
- 3 tablespoons fabulous olive oil
- 2 pinches sea salt

Make the sauce first. In a large frying pan, *simmer* olive oil and garlic with carrots, celery, and salt. *Stir* until roughly mixed and *add* tomatoes. *Simmer* slowly, blending the tomatoes with oil and vegetables. As the liquid evaporates, *stir* in the Zinfandel a little at a time. This is a labor of love, and it takes 3-4 hours of low heat to bring it all together into a sauce like consistency. As you achieve this, *turn* up heat to a fast simmer and *add* Carolina barbeque. *Stir* slowly and let meat and tomato sauce become one. This sauce can be refrigerated for up to four days. *Allow* sauce to return to room temperature before reheating. *Open* wine and pour yourself a glass. *Heat* 4-5 quarts of water. *Simmer* the sauce while boiling the pasta water, *sprinkle* the salt and *add* the pasta. *Stir* immediately. Despite what you've always been told watch the pot! *DON'T overcook* the pasta. It only takes 7-11 seconds after the water re-boils. *Drain* into colander as soon as possible. *Refill* your glass with Zinfandel. *Heat* sauce to a slow simmer for 14-18 minutes. *Coat* the serving dish with sauce, *pour* in noodles, *douse* with remainder of sauce. *Add* grated cheese and *toss*. *Add* a little fresh pepper on top and serve! *Share* the cooking wine with everyone ("cooking wine" is consumed while cooking). Buon appetito y'all!

Mushroom Truffle Spaghetti
by Isaac Mizrahi

INGREDIENTS

- *3 tablespoons extra virgin olive oil*
- *2 tablespoons unsalted butter*
- *1 large onion, chopped into matchsticks*
- *4 fat cloves garlic, minced*
- *8 cups mushrooms, any variety, cleaned, washed and sliced. Recommended: a blend of Shitake, Enoki, Porcini and Portobello*
- *1½ cups chicken stock*

- *1 pound spaghetti*
- *8 cups water*
- *2 tablespoons fresh sage, minced*
- *2 ½ tablespoons truffle paste*
- *⅓ cup cream*
- *salt to taste*
- *fresh ground pepper*
- *Pecorino Romano, grated for garnish*

Boil water with plenty of salt for the spaghetti. On medium-high heat, in a large frying pan, *heat* oil and butter. *Sauté* onion for 2-3 minutes until opaque. *Add* minced garlic, and *cook* for about one minute, *stirring* constantly, being careful not to burn it. *Mix* in mushrooms. (It may seem like a lot in the pan, but the mushrooms will reduce eventually. Also, if it seems like the oil and butter are absorbed too quickly by the mushrooms, don't worry, *add* another tablespoon or so of olive oil.) *Cook* for 3-5 minutes, adding ½ teaspoon of salt in the last stages. *Add* half of the sage, reserving the other half. *Increase* to high heat and *add* chicken stock. *Bring* to a boil, then *reduce* heat and simmer for 8 minutes. At this point, *drop* the spaghetti into the boiling water and *cook* for 8 minutes. (Note: *do not* cook it for the recommended 12 minutes, because it should be undercooked when it goes into the ragù.) After the mushroom mixture has been simmering for 5 minutes *add* truffle paste, and simmer for another minute. *Add* cream and simmer for the last 2 minutes. *Pull* the pasta from the water with tongs, *placing* the wet pasta directly into ragù. *Add* remaining sage, salt and pepper to taste and *simmer* for 2 more minutes. If the ragù seems dry, add the reserved starchy water as needed. *Serve* immediately and *garnish* each bowl with freshly grated Pecorino Romano.

❝I love this recipe because if you master this technique, you can improvise, substitute and make up recipes of your own. I made this pasta once for my mom and she still threatens to ask for the recipe.❞

Saffron Penne
by Rebecca Moses

INGREDIENTS
- *8 teaspoons butter*
- *extra virgin olive oil*
- *1 scallion finely chopped*
- *8 teaspoons grated Parmesan cheese*
- *12 ounces penne pasta*
- *6 ⅓ cups salted chicken stock*
- *1 saffron thread*

In a large pot, *melt* butter with 1 tablespoon extra virgin olive oil. *Add* chopped scallion and *cook* until translucent, about 10 minutes. *Add* the uncooked penne and stir until it absorbs the above ingredients. *Pour* in one ladle of stock, *stir* and let absorb. *Continue* like this, one ladle at a time (as though you were cooking risotto) until the pasta is done al dente in about 10-15 minutes, depending on the quality of the pasta. You should start *tasting* it after about 8-9 minutes of cooking time. Just before the pasta is ready (about 2 minutes) *add* the saffron dissolved in a cup of stock and stir. Take the pot off the heat and sprinkle the Parmesan cheese over the pasta and mix it well. *Serve* immediately.

Ricotta and Spinach Gnocchi
By Ralph Rucci

INGREDIENTS
- *2 cups spinach, chopped, mashed and drained (approximately 2 pounds fresh spinach)*
- *2 cups freshly grated Parmigiano-Reggiano cheese*
- *½ cup all-purpose flour*
- *1 cup whole-milk ricotta*
- *2 eggs*
- *pinch of nutmeg*
- *salt and pepper*
- *3 ounces butter, melted*

In mixing bowl, *combine* spinach with ½ cup of Parmigiano, ¼ cup of flour, ricotta, eggs, nutmeg, salt and pepper and mix well. *Take* chestnut-sized balls of the mixture and roll in remaining flour and *let* them settle for 30 minutes. *Bring* a large pot of water to a boil and *cook* a few at a time until they float to the surface. *Drain* well. To serve, *pour* melted butter over the gnocchi and *top* with Parmigiano-Reggiano.

The link between fashion and food is obvious.... creativity, passion, indulgence, the colors, the textures,.... fashionable food or just fabulous food? Oh! the creativity we can share while cooking... I am in a yellow state of mind.... think SAFFRON .... Warm gorgeous yellow... I'm thinking of my favorite food from my adopted country of Italy...

SAFFRON PASTA !!

Yummy! I love to think of new ways of preparing pasta.... Saffron Pasta is made in a completely different manner than normal pasta... we will cook it like we cook risotto... so get ready to make a delicious pasta your guests will never forget !!

Suggested Wine:

BARBERA D'ASTI
BRICCO
DELLO
BIGOTTA
PRODUCER-
BRAIDA-G.BOLOGNA
2004

OR

SAUVIGNON
SANCT VALENTIN
2007
FROM
TRENTINO
PRODUCER-
SAN MICHELE APPIANO

Suggested Flowers

YELLOW/RED
FEATHERED
TULIPS

Suggested Guests

Eclectic, interesting
and those who
Love to
eat and
drink and
enjoy life!

Suggested Music

PAOLO CONTE
BLUE SWING

Buon Appetito!

Buon Appetito!

Saturday Night Chicken
by Diane von Furstenberg

INGREDIENTS

- *1 or more whole chickens*
- *½ lemon*
- *sage leaves*
- *2 tablespoons sour cream*
- *2 tablespoons mustard of your choice*
- *potatoes*
- *rosemary*
- *olive oil*

Preheat oven to 400 degrees. *Wash*, *dry* and *salt* the chicken and *put* in a Pyrex baking dish. *Squeeze* the juice of ½ lemon inside chicken cavity. *Add* sage leaves (the more the better), sour cream and mustard inside the chicken. *Peel* potatoes and put in baking dish. *Sprinkle* rosemary and olive oil on chicken and potatoes. *Bake* at 400 degrees for 1 ½ hours. *Serve* it with love.

> **I have never been a great cook, yet when you cook for the ones you love, you somehow become one. My Saturday Night Chicken is a simple recipe, full of herbs and full of love. It is a meal that somehow is so cozy and delicious that you always end up eating it with your hands!**

Tagine of Chicken with Preserved Lemons and Olives by Yigal Azrouel

INGREDIENTS

- ¼ cup olive oil, plus 2 tablespoons
- 1 teaspoon cumin
- 1 teaspoon coriander
- 1 teaspoon sweet paprika
- ¼ teaspoon red pepper flakes
- ½ teaspoon saffron threads or powder
- ½ teaspoon cinnamon
- ¼ teaspoon ground cloves
- ¼ teaspoon ground ginger
- 1 4-pound chicken, cut into 8 pieces
- 2 onions, thinly sliced
- 1 garlic clove, minced
- 1 preserved lemon peel, sliced
- ½ cup green olives, pitted
- 1 ½ cups chicken stock
- ¼ teaspoon freshly ground black pepper
- 2 tablespoons fresh cilantro, minced
- 2 tablespoons fresh flat-leaf parsley, minced
- juice of 1/2 lemon

In a large bowl *combine* 1/4 cup olive oil, cumin, coriander, paprika, red pepper flakes, saffron, cinnamon, cloves and ginger. *Season* chicken with salt and pepper and add to marinade. *Stir* until marinade covers each piece. *Refrigerate* for 2 hours up to overnight. *Remove* chicken from marinade and *pat* dry. *Reserve* marinade. *Heat* remaining 2 tablespoons of olive oil in tagine or large Dutch oven. *Place* chicken skin side down in the hot oil and brown 4-5 minutes. *Turn* and *brown* other side for an additional 3-4 minutes. *Remove* chicken from tagine and *reserve* on a plate. *Add* onions and garlic and *saute* until tender, about 5 minutes. *Add* reserved marinade and chicken, lemon peel, green olives, stock and pepper. *Bring* to a low boil and *reduce* heat to a simmer. *Cover* and cook for 45 minutes. *Stir* in cilantro, parsley and lemon juice. *Transfer* to a serving platter and *serve* with couscous.

66 The recipe was originally from a friend of mine, Erez Sabag, who would make it for a group of us after surfing in Costa Rica. I love it because it's a one dish meal, it has a beautiful presentation and it introduces people to my heritage. 99

Arroz Con Pollo
by Stephen Dweck

INGREDIENTS

- 1 whole chicken, cut into 8 pieces (remove skin, if desired)
- ¼ cup olive oil
- 2 large onions, chopped
- 6 cloves of garlic, diced
- 1 large green pepper, chopped
- 4 plum tomatoes (canned whole tomatoes), chopped
- ½ jalapeno pepper, seeds removed, chopped finely
- 2 bay leaves
- 1 packet of Goya Sazon seasoning
- 1 teaspoon oregano
- ½ teaspoon salt
- 1/3 cup green olives, pitted
- 2 cups water
- 2 cups parboiled rice
- 1 can beer
- 4 tablespoons cider vinegar
- roasted red peppers
- frozen peas, thawed
- capers

Place onions, tomatoes, green peppers, jalapeno pepper and garlic in a wide, shallow pot. *Add* capers, green olives, bay leaves, oregano and olive oil. *Saute* for 15 minutes until stew-like. *Add* chicken, water, and vinegar. *Cover* and simmer until chicken is tender. *Don't* overcook. *Remove* chicken and set aside. *Add* rice to vegetable mixture and *simmer* uncovered until water is absorbed then *add* 1 can of beer. *Cover* and simmer until rice is soft. To serve, *place* rice on a large platter or serving dish. *Place* chicken over rice and *garnish* with roasted red peppers and green peas.

Favorite Baked/Rotisserie Chicken
by Brian Reyes

INGREDIENTS

- 2 3-to-4 pound chickens
- ½ red bell pepper
- ½ green pepper
- ½ Spanish onion
- 3 green onions or scallions
- 3 garlic cloves
- 1 tablespoon Goya Sazon (cilantro and achiote)
- 1 tablespoon Goya Adobo with pepper
- 3 bay leaves
- 1 teaspoon fresh thyme
- 1 teaspoon cumin
- 1 teaspoon fresh ground black pepper
- 3 tablespoons olive oil
- 3 tablespoons ketchup
- 1 beer
- ½ glass red wine
- salt to taste

Mix ingredients above in a blender or food processor until consistency is a liquid marinade. *Place* the whole chickens in marinade bag or container and pour the marinade inside and outside of each chicken. *Marinate* each chicken for 24 hours. To bake, *preheat* oven to 350 degrees. *Place* the chickens in a baking pan and *bake* at 350 degrees for 1 hour, *basting* occasionally. Do not cover the chickens. After the hour has passed, *broil* chickens for another 10-15 minutes, until chickens are a golden brown. To roast in rotisserie, *place* chickens onto a spit and *set* the grill on medium temperature. *Close* lid and *cook* for 1 to 1 ½ hours, or until the internal temperature reaches 180 degrees (check each thigh). *Remove* chickens from grill and *let stand* for 10-15 minutes before cutting into pieces and serving.

"This is my favorite dish that my family used to cook at our restaurant in New Jersey. The restaurant has since closed, but I try to make it whenever I can. We love to have it for family parties over the summer—it's best served outside with plenty of napkins."

Sicilian Chicken with Olives and Capers
by Geri Gerard

INGREDIENTS

- *3 ½ pounds chicken legs and thighs*
- *3 celery stalks, sliced in 1/2 -inch pieces*
- *4-5 garlic cloves, sliced thin*
- *1 cup Sicilian green olives, cut in half and pitted*
- *1 cup kalamata olives, cut in half and pitted*
- *4 tablespoons capers*
- *vegetable oil*
- *chicken broth*
- *rice*

Sauté chicken in heavy cast-iron skillet with warm oil until lightly browned. *Remove* from skillet, *set* aside on plate and *cover* to keep warm. *Add* garlic to the skillet and *sauté*, adding more oil if necessary. When soft, *add* celery, olives and capers to the pan. *Sauté* for 3 minutes. *Put* chicken back in the skillet. *Add* enough chicken broth to cover halfway up the pan. *Cover* and *simmer* on low heat for approximately 30-45 minutes until chicken is done. *Serve* over a bed of rice.

Dad's Fabulous Curried Chicken with Golden Eggs by Zang Toi

INGREDIENTS

- *13 quail eggs, hard-boiled*
- *2 ¼ cups corn oil*
- *½ cup jasmine rice*
- *2 shallots, finely minced*
- *4 tablespoons curry powder*
- *2 tablespoons salt*
- *1 stalk lemongrass, chopped*
- *1 large chicken, cut into 13 pieces*
- *1 tablespoon sugar*
- *7 small red chili peppers*
- *3 cups coconut milk*

Peel quail eggs, then *deep fry* in about 2 cups oil until golden brown. *Set aside*. *Toast* rice in a frying pan over medium heat, then *grind* into medium fine powder. *Set* aside. In a wok or large pot, *heat* remaining ¼ cup of oil and *brown* minced shallots over medium heat. *Add* curry powder, salt and lemongrass. *Cook*, gently stirring, until golden brown. *Add* chicken, sugar and chili peppers, ¼ cup coconut milk and browned rice powder. *Cook* 7 minutes stirring constantly, then add 2 ¼ cups coconut milk. *Bring* to a rapid boil, reduce heat and simmer 40 minutes. *Stir* in remaining ½ cup coconut milk and the eggs. *Cook* over medium heat 13 minutes.

Cornish Game Hens with Truffle Oil
by Katrin Zimmermann, *Ex Ovo*

INGREDIENTS

- *2 Cornish game hens*
- *3 tablespoons black truffle oil, per bird*
- *salt and pepper*
- *kitchen twine*

Preheat oven to 500 degrees. *Rinse* and pat dry Cornish game hens, *salt and pepper* inside and out, *place* on roasting pan with wire pan grate. *Apply* drops of truffle oil onto birds, *rub* into the skin and into the cavity. *Loosen* the skin that covers the breasts by slowly pushing your fingers between meat and skin. *Fill* with truffle oil, push in with finger and *massage* meat underneath the skin; try to *push* as far as the legs. The more truffle oil, the more decadent. *Tie* legs with kitchen twine. *Roast* hens at 500 degrees for 10-12 minutes, then *turn* down oven to 400 degrees and *roast* for 40 minutes more. *Serve* with truffled asparagus and wild rice.

Iron-Skillet Twice Fried Chicken
by Nicholas Varney

INGREDIENTS

- *1 2 ½-to-3 pound chicken, cut into pieces*
- *bacon fat or lard, enough to half fill a cast-iron skillet*
- *1 cup all-purpose flour*
- *1 teaspoon coarse sea salt*
- *½ teaspoon Zanzibar black pepper, cracked*
- *cayenne pepper*
- *brown paper bag*

Wash the chicken parts thoroughly and *dry* them on paper towels. *Place* chicken in the refrigerator for 30 minutes to dry out the skin. There's no wetness permitted when applying the flour mixture or when frying the bird. *Heat* fat to approximately 380 degrees in a heavy cast-iron skillet. *Mix* together flour, salt, pepper and a healthy dose of cayenne pepper so the mix has a light pink hue and place mixture in a big brown paper bag. *Add* the chicken pieces, a few at a time, and shake well to ensure that each piece is coated with the seasoned flour. *Fry* chicken uncovered for 2 minutes, turning until golden brown on all sides. The pieces will not yet be cooked through. *Remove* chicken pieces and dry off with paper towel and *put* back in fridge to dry off more (5 minutes). *Recoat* chicken with flour mix. *Place* in iron skillet again and *fry* until cooked through, about 20-25 minutes. *Drain* on paper towels. *Double* frying the chicken creates a fried "shell" which keeps the chicken moist and tender inside. The cast-iron skillet retains the heat necessary to seal the chicken and crisp the skin.

> ❝At my first trunk show ever at the Macon, Georgia Cherry Blossom Festival, I was told any proper young man should be able to prepare a meal he could be proud of and share with his lady friends. After much discussion with many of the Magnolias perusing the Uchino Cherry trees in blossom, I took my own liberties with the bird and now cook the greatest fried chicken of all time. The key to the recipe is twofold; an iron skillet and lard. Without either of the two, the recipe fails.❞

Ginger Beef
by Reed Krakoff, *Coach*
Courtesy of Karen Lee

INGREDIENTS
- *1 pound filet of beef, trimmed of fat and silver*
  (or end-cut sirloin,flank steak or skirt steak)

MARINADE
- *1 tablespoon light soy sauce*
- *1 ½ teaspoons sugar*
- *1 teaspoon water chestnut powder*

SEASONING SAUCE
- *1 teaspoon water chestnut powder*
- *2 tablespoons sherry*
- *1 ½ tablespoons Chinese dark soy sauce*
- *2 tablespoons ginger, finely shredded*
- *½ cup scallion, shredded (whites and green parts)*
- *3 tablespoons pure olive oil, extra virgin olive oil*
  or peanut oil
- *10 more V-cut snow peas, for garnish, blanched*

Slice steak into 3/8 inch thick pieces. *Place* beef and ingredients for marinade in a bowl and stir with chopsticks. *Refrigerate* while preparing the rest of the recipe. To prepare sauce, *dissolve* 1 teaspoon water chestnut powder in sherry, and combine with remainder of sauce ingredients. *Place* a wok over high heat to 2-3 minutes or until it smokes. *Add* oil and heat a few seconds. *Place* half of beef in the wok in a single layer. *Saute* about 30 seconds or until it is nicely seared. Working quickly, *turn* each piece of meat and sear another 20-30 seconds. *Remove* the beef from the wok, allowing the fat to drain back into the wok. *Place* beef on serving dish. *Repeat* the frying procedure with the remaining beef and remove from the wok. In the remaining oil, *stir fry* the ginger and scallion for one minute over high heat. *Stir* the seasoning sauce and *add* it to the wok with all of the beef; *stir fry* for about 30 seconds. *Empty* the contents of the wok into a heated serving dish and *serve* immediately. *Garnish* with blanched snow peas around the beef or a few shredded scallions on top.

Swedish Sandwich Tart
by Richard Bengtsson

INGREDIENTS

- 1 loaf white bread, crusts removed
- mayonnaise
- 8 ounces liver paté
- 4 ounces blue cheese, crumbled
- 8 ounces sliced Swiss cheese or any sliced cheese of your choice
- ½ pound sliced turkey
- ½ pound sliced ham
- 4 ounces salad shrimp
- 1 pint whipping cream
- 7 tablespoons mayonnaise
- salt
- Green, leafy lettuce
- 1 hothouse (English) cucumber
- 4 ounces salad shrimp
- 2 hard-boiled eggs, sliced into thin rounds
- 2 tomatoes, diced
- 2 tablespoons fresh dill, chopped
- 2 tablespoons fresh parsley, chopped

Construct the bottom of the sandwich tart by placing four slices of bread in a square on a small wooden cutting board (or other serving plate of your choice). On the left side of the square, *place* a halved piece of bread next to the upper left and another halved piece next to the lower left whole piece of bread. You should end up with a rectangle that is two pieces of bread deep and 2 ½ pieces long. This is the base of the tart. *Cover* the bottom layer of the tart with 8 ounces of liver pate. *Sprinkle* 4 ounces of blue cheese on top of the liver paté, equally distributed across the tart. For the second layer of the tart, *do* exactly as you did for the bottom level, except *place* the halved pieces of crustless bread to the right of the tart. This creates a reinforced structure, similar to how masons make a brick wall. The second tier of the tart should also be two bread pieces deep and 2 ½ pieces long. *Cover* the second tier of the tart with a thin layer of mayonnaise. This serves three purposes: to moisten the bread, to adhere the tart together and for flavor. *Layer* 8 ounces of sliced Swiss cheese (or another cheese of your choice) on top of the mayonnaise-moistened bread. *Construct* the third tier of your tart just as you did the base. *Moisten* the third tier with a thin layer of mayonnaise. *Layer* 8 ounces of sliced turkey. *Construct* the fourth layer of your tart as you did the second layer, with the reinforcements on the right. *Layer* 8 ounces of sliced ham. *Construct* the fifth layer of crustless bread, and layer with salad shrimp. *Top* the shrimp layer with another layer of crustless bread, remembering to *alternate* the side for the extra halves. You should have five layers of sandwich fillings and six layers of bread. To make the tart's topping, *whip* one pint of whipping cream using an electric mixer until it begins to stiffen. *Add* 7 tablespoons of mayonnaise gradually and *whip* the cream until it forms soft peaks. *Add* a pinch of salt and mix. *Spread* the whipped cream and mayonnaise mixture on top of the sandwich tart as if it were a cake. *Cover* the top and all sides with the mixture. *Place* one layer of lettuce on top of your tart. *Follow* with the salad shrimp, sliced eggs and tomatoes, laying each topping in vertical strips across the tart from left to right. *Place* the slices of cucumber on the sides of the tart, anchoring each slice into the cream and mayonnaise topping. *Sprinkle* 2 tablespoons of chopped parsley and 2 tablespoons of chopped dill over the entire tart as a garnish. *Place* uncovered, into the refrigerator for up to six hours. For more than six hours, *cover* with plastic wrap. It can be stored up to 48 hours. *Serve* sliced as if it were cake.

"This is a wonderful and unique recipe for any group gathering. We've taken this classic Swedish dish and updated it using American flavors. The beauty of this dish lies, like most things Scandinavian, in its simplicity and versatility. Feel free to add or remove any fillings—it is truly a dish with which you can express your personal taste and artistic abilities. We must admit, half the fun comes from decorating the tart. The other half, however, is purely in eating it. Be sure to make it ahead so the bread becomes moist and the flavors meld.**"**

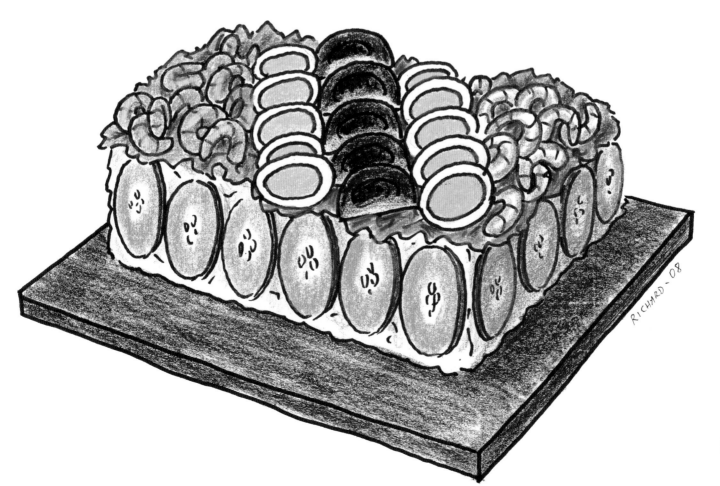

Stuffed Veal Roll Falso Magro al Sugo
by Carolina Amato

INGREDIENTS

- 1 ½ pounds veal, in one large cutlet-like slice
- ¼ pound ground veal
- 2 hard boiled eggs, chopped fine
- ¼ cup caciocavallo, grated
- 1 ¼ cups bread crumbs
- 1 raw egg
- 2 ounces provolone cheese, sliced
- 2 ounces mortadella, cut in fine slices
- 6 tablespoons olive oil
- 1 clove garlic, chopped fine
- 1 onion, chopped fine
- 1 stalk celery, chopped fine
- 1 carrot, chopped fine
- 2 heaping tablespoons tomato paste
- 16 ounce can chopped tomatoes
- 1 clove
- freshly grated nutmeg
- 2/3 cup dry red wine

Pound veal slice to make one large, pliable sheet of thin meat. You can *splice* two pieces together if necessary. *Place* the sheet of meat on a wet cloth. *Mix* ground veal with chopped egg, bread crumbs, cacciocavalo cheese and bind together with raw egg. *Season* with salt, pepper and nutmeg. *Spread* the stuffing over the veal cutlet leaving a border around the edges. *Cover* the stuffing with provolone and mortadella. *Roll* the meat up like a jellyroll and try to close the ends. *Secure* with kitchen string. *Heat* the olive oil in a large, deep frying pan and add the garlic, onion, celery and carrot. *Sauté* until softened and translucent. *Stir* in the tomato paste and then the chopped tomatoes. *Add* clove and nutmeg and simmer gently for fifteen minutes. *Lay* the meat roll in the pan and spoon the sauce over it as though you were basting the meat. *Add* the red wine, allowing the alcohol to evaporate, then *add* enough water to cover the meat. *Cover* and simmer very gently for about 30 minutes. *Check* the pan often and make sure that the meat is not sticking to the pan. To serve, *remove* the string from the meat and slice. *Reduce* the sauce to half its volume. *Serve* the sauce in a gravy boat or drizzle it over the slices.

“ This veal dish is excellent for a dinner party or buffet because it can be prepared in advance and served either warm or at room temperature. It pairs well with either risotto or polenta. It's a unique dish, rarely seen in a restaurant, and offers a complex blend of flavors. ”

Grandma Bea's Pot Roast
by Michael Kors

INGREDIENTS

- olive oil
- 5 pounds flat-cut brisket
- salt and pepper
- garlic powder
- paprika
- 16 ounce can, tomatoes
- 1 large onion, sliced
- 2 bay leaves
- 1 green pepper, chopped
- 4-6 carrots, sliced ¾ -inch long
- 4-6 celery stalks, sliced ¾ -inch long
- ½ pound mushrooms, sliced
- 1 cup dry red wine

Spread a thin film of olive oil in a Dutch oven and heat it on stove top. *Sear* the brisket on high heat, browning on both sides. *Season* lightly with salt, pepper, garlic powder and paprika on both sides. *Add* tomatoes, onions, bay leaves and wine. *Bring* to a boil, cover and reduce heat. *Simmer* for 2 hours. *Add* green pepper, celery and carrots. *Cook* for 1 hour longer, or until meat and vegetables are fork-tender. *Add* mushrooms for the last 30 minutes of cooking time. *Slice* meat across the grain and moisten sliced meat with tomato sauce. *Serve* surrounded by vegetables on a bed of wide noodles. *Pass* remaining sauce in a gravy boat.

66 It's chunky, hearty and cozy—a meal version of a ten-ply cashmere turtleneck. 99

Grilled Lamb Chops with Fresh Mint
by Elie Tahari

INGREDIENTS

- *3 racks of lamb, Frenched*
- *olive oil*
- *salt and pepper*
- *1 bunch fresh mint leaves, cut into long, thin strips (chiffonade)*
- *1 cup sugar*
- *1 cup Champagne vinegar*
- *1 cup water*

Cut racks of lamb into chops *Brush* with olive oil and salt and pepper. *Set* aside. *Chiffonade cut* the fresh mint. *Mix* it with sugar, vinegar and water. *Let* this mixture sit for at least a half hour or until sugar dissolves. *Grill* lamb chops on a charcoal grill or a very hot sauté pan. *Brown* well on both sides or until chops are medium rare. *Transfer* to a large platter and dress with mint sauce. *Garnish* with a sprig of fresh mint. *Serve* immediately.

"Every time we cook it, which is often, the whole family enjoys it. The kids love it because they can hold the bone and eat it. Make sure the lamb chops have a minimal amount of fat— that's how we like it."

Veal Milanese and River Salad
by Dennis Basso

INGREDIENTS

- 8 large veal cutlets, pounded
- 1 cup unseasoned bread crumbs
- ½ cup Parmesan cheese
- 1 cup all-purpose flour
- ¼ cup olive oil
- 2 garlic cloves, minced
- ¼ cup flat parsley, finely chopped
- salt, pepper
- 4 eggs, beaten

RIVER SALAD

- 1 large bunch baby arugula, washed and stems removed
- 1 small red onion, peeled and sliced into long, thin slivers
- fresh Parmesan cheese flakes
- juice of one large lemon
- salt and freshly ground black pepper

In a shallow pan, *mix* flour with salt and pepper to taste. *Mix* bread crumbs, garlic, parsley and cheese in a second pan. Generously *salt and pepper*. *Put* beaten eggs in a third pan. *Dredge* veal through flour, *dip* in the egg wash and then *place* in the breadcrumb mixture pan. *Pat* firmly on both sides until coated. *Place* on a plate. *Put* frying pan over medium heat and heat olive oil until almost bubbly. *Cook* each veal cutlet 4-5 minutes per side until golden brown. *Remove* and drain on paper towels to blot excess oil. *Garnish* with lemon wedges. Top with *River Salad*.

RIVER SALAD

In a mixing bowl, *combine* olive oil, lemon juice, salt and pepper by stirring mixture after each item is added. *Place* arugula and onion in mixing bowl, *add* dressing and toss.
Top with Parmesan flakes. *Serve* on top of veal cutlets or as a side dish.

> " This is a favorite at our house served with River Salad on top and on the side eaten together. The combination of the crispy veal and the cool taste of the River Salad is the perfect bite combination. "

Osso Bucco
by Patricia Von Musulin

INGREDIENTS

- 3 whole garlic cloves
- 2 bay leaves
- 1 small sprig fresh thyme
- 2 sprigs fresh rosemary
- 4 whole veal shanks cut about 4 inches long (approximately 1 pound per shank)
- sea salt
- ½ cup all-purpose flour
- ½ cup extra virgin olive oil
- carrots, cut into 1 inch pieces
- small onions, cut into quarters
- 1 stalk celery, cut into diagonal slices ¾ inch
- 2 tomatoes, cut into small cubes and mashed to a pulp
- 4 tablespoons fresh Italian parsley, chopped
- several sprigs, fresh Italian parsley
- 1 ½ cups dry, white Italian wine
- 2 cups chicken stock
- kitchen twine

Assemble veal shanks on a dry surface and *wipe* lightly to remove any excess water or juices. *Wrap* each shank with kitchen twine to secure the meat to the bone. *Sprinkle* the wrapped shanks with fresh pepper and *salt* lightly. *Roll* in all-purpose flour and dust off any excess. *Place* olive oil into a Dutch oven, or a large, heavy pan, and heat it on the stove. *Add* veal shanks, turning them often so that they are uniformly browned. *Remove* shanks and place garlic, carrots, onions, and celery in pot. *Sprinkle* with sea salt and fresh pepper and *sauté* for about 6 minutes until soft. *Add* the diced and mashed tomatoes and replace the veal shanks into the Dutch oven. *Add* white wine, Italian parsley, bay leaves, rosemary, thyme, and chicken stock. *Simmer* for 1 hour. *Remove* the shanks and assemble on a serving platter. The meat should be tender and falling off the bone. *Place* the vegetables on the serving platter and *garnish* with sprigs of fresh parsley.

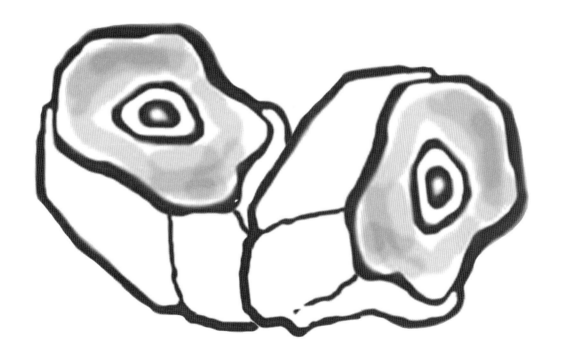

Richard's Crab Cake

Maryland Crab Cakes
by Richard Lambertson, *Lambertson Truex*

INGREDIENTS
- *2 pounds Maryland lump crab meat*
- *1 large egg*
- *¾ cup mayonnaise (no substitutes!)*
- *2 tablespoons whole grain mustard*
- *¾ teaspoon coarse salt*
- *½ teaspoon fresh ground black pepper*
- *½ cup cilantro leaves, chopped*
- *2 scallions, finely chopped*
- *½ medium red bell pepper, finely diced (if using a large pepper just use ¼ of it)*
- *½ cup finely crumbled saltine crackers*
- *lemon wedges*
- *side of mixed greens (optional)*

Preheat the oven to 400 degrees. *Lightly* oil a baking sheet. *Pick* over the crabmeat and *remove* cartilage, being careful *not to break* up the lumps too much. *Set* aside in a medium bowl. In a large bowl, *whisk* egg until blended. *Add* mayonnaise, mustard, salt and pepper and whisk until smooth. *Add* the cilantro, scallions and bell pepper and mix well. *Fold* in crabmeat and saltines with a rubber spatula, being careful not to break up the lumps of crab. Gently *form* the crabmeat mixture into cakes that are 2 inches in diameter and 1 inch thick. *Place* the cakes on the prepared baking sheet. *Bake* at 400 degrees for about 15 minutes or until lightly golden, carefully *turning* once with a metal spatula during baking so the crab cakes don't stick. *Remove* crab cakes from oven and set aside on baking sheet or wire rack. They can rest here as you prepare other parts of your dinner. Just before serving, *preheat* the oven to broil and move the rack close to the broiler. *Watch* your crabcakes brown just a bit more. *Remove* from the broiler, *cover* loosely with aluminum foil to keep warm. To *serve*, *arrange* on a plate with mixed greens. *Add* lemon wedges. *Enjoy*!

> 66 I made up this recipe from three different sources and have perfected it over time. I've been making it for about 10 years. These crab cakes make a great lunch or first course served on a bed of lettuce, or even better, made bite-size for cocktail parties.99

Scallops Flambé with Whiskey
by Roland Nivelais

INGREDIENTS
- *½ pound sea scallops*
- *whiskey*
- *crème frâiche*
- *salt and pepper*
- *salted butter from Brittany region of France*
- *linguine*

Place sea scallops in a pan with a 2 teaspoons of crème frâiche. *Add* salt and pepper, then *sauté* for about 5 minutes. *Set* aside. *Pour* 3 tablespoons of whiskey into a pan, *warm* to just under a boil. *Once* whisky is warmed, *take* a match and light whiskey to get flambé effect. Carefully (watch your hairsprayed 'do!) *pour* whisky reduction onto the scallops and *sauté* in pan until brown. *Serve* on a bed of linguine with a pat of salty butter from Brittany.

Mussels in Tomato and Heavy Cream
by Stephen Burrows

INGREDIENTS
- *2 pounds mussels, cleaned and de-bearded*
- *4 cloves garlic, smashed and roughly chopped*
- *1 can tomatoes sauce with basil (or your favorite kind of homemade sauce)*
- *olive oil*
- *¼ cup white wine*
- *2 tablespoons Smart Balance buttery spread*
- *¼ pint heavy cream (or fat free half and half)*
- *sea salt*

Place mussels and all ingredients (except heavy cream) into sauce pot. *Cook* mussels on medium heat until they open (approximately 7-10 minutes) and *remove* from heat. *Add* heavy cream, *stir* and *serve* immediately. This is great served over thin spaghetti.

Shrimp in Yuca and Coconut Cream Sauce by Francisco Costa, *Calvin Klein*

INGREDIENTS

- *4 pounds fresh medium size shrimp*
- *2 pounds Yuca, peeled and washed (also know as Mandioca, a Brazilian starch root)*
- *2 pounds tomatoes, well ripened*
- *1 can coconut milk (500 ml. or 2 cups)*
- *1 can heavy cream ("crème de leite" remove the excess liquid from top)*
- *2 tablespoons palm oil*
- *1 teaspoon olive oil*
- *2 onions*
- *1 clove garlic*
- *1 bunch of parsley*
- *salt and pepper to taste*

In a skillet, *heat* the olive oil and *sauté* onions, garlic, parsley and add pepper to taste. *Blend* the tomatoes in a food processor and add to skillet. *Let* everything cook in the skillet until softened. In a separate pot, *boil* the peeled yuca until it becomes lightly tender and soft enough to put a fork through it, between 20-30 minutes. *Add* the shrimp to the skillet mixture and cook for 10 minutes on high heat. Once the shrimp is cooked, *add* in the yuca, stirring so that it is well incorporated into the mixture. *Add* coconut milk and heavy cream. *Salt* to taste.

66I got this recipe from a friend in Salvador da Bahia, Brazil, who happens to be a wonderful chef. I like this dish because it represents a typical Brazilian style of cooking and embodies all the rich, spicy, diverse flavors of my culture.99

Fun Szi Cellophane Noodles with Chinese Sausage and Prawns by Amy 8 Chan

INGREDIENTS

- ½ pound cellophane noodles
- 1 cucumber
- ¼ inch ginger, chopped
- 1 Chinese sweet sausage
- 1 Chinese duck sausage
- 1 pound prawns

- soy sauce
- ginger slices
- 2 teaspoon canola oil
- ½ cup organic chicken broth
- scallions (for garnish)
- about 2 tablespoons white wine

Soak cellophane noodles in water for five minutes, *drain*. *Slice* cucumber into skinny threads. *Blanche* Chinese sausages and *drain* the fat. *Slice* into ¼-inch pieces. *Clean*, *devein* and *butterfly* the prawns. *Marinate* in soy sauce and ginger. *Add* 2 teaspoons canola oil to a deep pan and brown sausages until crisp, *remove* and *set aside*. *Quickly* sauté prawns and sliced ginger in pan, *add* a splash of white wine and then *take* the prawns out when they begin to curl. *Add* ¼ teaspoon canola oil to pan, *cook* cellophane noodles for three minutes while stirring. *Add* chicken broth and *cook* until liquid is absorbed. *Toss* in prawns and sausages, top with cucumber and scallions (crushed peanuts optional) and *serve*.

Simplest Sole Meuniere
by Laura Poretzky, *Abaete*

INGREDIENTS

- 1 filet of sole per person (Either get gray sole or Dover sole. They taste a little different, but just get the one that seems the freshest.)
- white flour

- fresh parsley, chopped fine
- 4 tablespoons good butter
- salt and pepper
- lemon wedges

Dredge the fish in flour, *shake* off the excess flour, and *set* aside. In the meantime *heat* the butter and parsley in a sauté pan until hot, almost browned. *Use* enough butter to cover the bottom of the pan. *Do* not reuse butter. If you need to use the pan twice, then *change* the butter. *Add* the fish and cook on each side until slightly browned, about 3 minutes each side. *Put* the fish on a serving plate. *Take* the remaining butter from the pan, *add* some lemon juice, and put mixture on top of fish. *Season* with salt and pepper. *Sprinkle* some fresh parsley on top, and voila! *Serve* this with the simplest steamed potatoes, and a good bottle of Chardonnay. Everybody will be pleased.

Crabmeat Maryland
by Marcia Sherrill

Courtesy of Lily Peavers

INGREDIENTS

- ¼ cup butter
- 3 tablespoons flour
- 2 cups milk
- 2 tablespoons onion, minced
- ½ teaspoon celery salt
- ¾ teaspoon orange peel, grated
- 1 tablespoon parsley, minced
- 1 tablespoon green pepper, minced
- 1 pimento, minced

- ½ teaspoon Crystal hot sauce
- ¼ cup dry sherry
- 1 egg, beaten
- 1 teaspoon salt
- ¼ teaspoon pepper
- 3 cups fresh crabmeat, picked over for shells
- ½ cup soft breadcrumbs
- 1 tablespoon butter, melted

Preheat oven to 350 degrees. *Melt* butter, stir in flour and *cook* for 1 to 2 minutes. *Stir* in milk and *whisk* until thickened. *Add* onion and the next six ingredients. *Remove* from heat and add sherry. *Stir* sauce slowly into beaten egg. *Add* salt, pepper, and crabmeat. *Place* into greased 1 ½ quart casserole. *Sprinkle* with crumbs mixed with melted butter. *Bake* at 350 for 15 to 20 minutes or until brown.

Paella
by Monique Lhuillier

INGREDIENTS

- *2 tablespoons olive oil*
- *1 medium onion, chopped*
- *1 medium or large red bell pepper, diced*
- *2 large garlic cloves, minced*
- *2 ½ cups long grain rice*
- *3 ½ cups fish broth or chicken broth*
- *¾ cup white wine*
- *2 teaspoons kosher salt, less if broth is salted*
- *12 large shrimp, peeled and deveined*
- *12 small clams, thoroughly scrubbed and rinsed*
- *12 black mussels, thoroughly scrubbed and rinsed*
- *½ cup tender young peas, fresh or frozen*
- *2 tablespoons fresh flat-leaf parsley, chopped, plus more for garnish*
- *generous ½ to ¾ teaspoon saffron threads (to taste), crushed with your fingers*
- *pinch of freshly ground black pepper*
- *pinch of cayenne*

Heat the oil over medium heat in a large, heavy skillet, and *add* the onion and red pepper. *Cook, stirring,* until onion is translucent, about 3 minutes. *Stir* in garlic and rice and continue to stir together for about 1 minute until the rice is coated with oil. *Add* the broth and wine and bring to a full boil over medium-high heat. *Add* all the other ingredients, reduce the heat and simmer 15 to 20 minutes until all of the liquid has evaporated and the rice is tender and beginning to stick to the pan. *Turn* off the heat and leave contents undisturbed for 10 minutes. *Stir* the mixture briefly to distribute the ingredients evenly. *Serve* in shallow serving bowls or plates, *garnish* with parsley.

"This is a recipe from my dear friend and chef extraordinaire, Wolfgang Puck."

Panang Assam Laksa
by Yeohlee Teng

INGREDIENTS

- *thumb size belachan, dried shrimp paste, toasted*
- *4 dried chilies*
- *2 fresh chilies*
- *1 stalk lemongrass*
- *2 shallots*
- *thumb size fresh tumeric*
- *1 piece tamarind pulp*
- *2 pieces tamarind peel*
- *1 stalk polygonal leaf (optional)*
- *5 cups water*
- *2 fresh mackerels with heads*

GARNISH

- *1 cucumber, peeled and cored seeds, sliced in to thin strips*
- *1 ginger flower (optional), shredded*
- *2 to 3 stalks mint, clean and separate leaves*
- *pineapple, sliced into thin strips*
- *mint leaves*
- *2 red onions, peeled and sliced*
- *2 red chilis, sliced thinly*

Combine all the ingredients but the fish and *simmer* over low heat until fragrant, about 20 minutes. *Season* to taste with salt and sugar. *Add* 1 cup of water and the 2 fish. *Simmer* for another 10-15 minutes. *Take* the fish out and separate the meat, discard head and bones. *Make* sauce by dissolving 1 tablespoon of black prawn paste in 2 tablespoons of hot water. *Prepare* vermicelli or spaghetti # 9 according to directions on the package. *Put* cooked noodles into 2 bowls, garnish with pineapple, cucumber, mint leaves, ginger flower, onions and chilies. *Add* flaked fish meat. *Top* with sauce of dissolved prawn paste, according to taste. *Add* fish broth.

Tilapia with Olive Risotto
by Doo-Ri Chung

INGREDIENTS

- *4 6-ounce tilapia fillets*
- *small bunch thyme*
- *olive oil*
- *salt and pepper*
- *¼ cup balsamic vinegar*
- *5 cups chicken stock*
- *tomato paste*
- *small onion, chopped*
- *1 cup Arborio rice*
- *½ cup dry white wine*
- *¼ cup Gaeta olives, chopped*
- *¼ cup Parmesan cheese, freshly grated*
- *1 tablespoon butter*

Sprinkle fillets with thyme, salt and pepper. *Fold* each fillet into thirds, placing a thyme sprig in between the folds. *Refrigerate.* In a small saucepan, *simmer* vinegar until it reduces to a tablespoon. *Set* aside. In a medium saucepan, *bring* the stock to a simmer and tomato paste. *Cover* and keep warm. *Heat* 2 tablespoons of olive oil in a large saucepan. *Add* onion and cook over low heat until softened. *Stir* in rice. *Add* the wine. *Simmer* over moderate heat until liquid is absorbed. *Add* 1 cup of stock, stirring constantly until liquid is absorbed. *Repeat* until the risotto is creamy and al dente—about 20 minutes. *Cover* risotto and keep it warm. In a medium skillet, heat remaining 2 tablespoons of olive oil. *Place* tilapia in pan, folded side down. *Cook* over moderate low heat until fish is browned at the bottom. *Turn* fish over and repeat until the fish is white throughout.

Rewarm risotto over moderate heat. *Stir* in ¼ cup stock. *Add* olives, Parmesan cheese and 1 tablespoon of butter. *Season* with salt and pepper. *Spoon* risotto into shallow bowls, *set* fish on top and *drizzle* the reduced balsamic vinegar on top of fish.

“ I have an ongoing folder of recipes torn from different magazines. Some I never get to and there are some I use over and over. This risotto recipe is one of those. It is from *Food & Wine* magazine many years ago. The original recipe called for lemon sole but I started using tilapia because the lemon sole always broke apart unless you used a lot of butter. The risotto is also something you can vary. ”

Rustic Spinach Pie
by Andrew Fezza

INGREDIENTS

- *2-3 pounds spinach, stalks trimmed*
- *½ cup extra virgin olive oil*
- *½ cup fresh basil leaves, loosely chopped*
- *1 ½ cups freshly grated Parmesan cheese*
- *2 cups all-purpose flour*
- *2 tablespoons lard or shortening*
- *salt*
- *olive oil*

Wash spinach, dry it thoroughly and put it in an extra large mixing bowl. *Sprinkle* lightly with salt and mix. *Add* oil, basil, and cheese and mix together evenly. *Set* mixture aside. *Mix* the flour and lard with 8 tablespoons of cold water in a medium sized mixing bowl. *Knead* into fairly stiff dough. *When* finished divide dough into 2 pieces. *Generously* grease a 10-inch pie pan (preferably ceramic) with olive oil. *Roll* out one piece of dough as thin as possible and line the greased pan with it. *Fill* the pan with the spinach and gently pat down into a dome shape within the pan. *Roll* out the second piece of dough as thin as possible and *place* it loosely on top of the spinach pie. Now for the creativity—*drape* the top layer of dough, adding decorative touches within the folds of the dough. *Pinch* the edges together around the pie pan. You can *fold* back any extra dough onto the surface of your pie or you can cut off any extra pieces and add them as decorative appliques on the pie surface. Once you are finished with your design, take a sharp kitchen knife and *poke* a few tiny holes in the pie surface to allow steam to escape while cooking. *Brush* finished pie with olive oil and bake in oven at 350 degrees for about 1 hour, checking every 15 minutes. *Drizzle* surface with olive oil as needed during cooking (usually once or twice). Finished surface should be bronzed and beautiful but not burnt. *Cut* into slices and serve hot or at room temperature. The spinach will shrink down while cooking and the dome shape may settle slightly. The beauty of this pie is in its individuality!

Mom's Jiffy Eggplant Parmigiana
by Mary Ann Restivo

INGREDIENTS

- 2 small Italian eggplants
- 2 cloves garlic, peeled
- olive oil
- 2 tablespoons all-purpose flour
- 1 teaspoon salt

- 1 teaspoon sugar
- ¼ pound fresh ricotta cheese
- dried oregano
- Parmesan cheese, grated
- simple tomato sauce, simmered

Sift flour, salt and sugar into a bowl. *Wash* and dry the eggplants. *Remove* both ends of the eggplants and cut into 1-inch rounds with the skin on. *Heat* a generous layer of olive oil in a metal frying pan with the garlic cloves. *Dip* each piece of eggplant into the flour mixture, covering both sides. When oil is hot, *place* eggplant into the pan and *brown* on both sides, cooking until it's soft in the center, about 10 minutes. *Remove* browned eggplant and *drain* on paper towels. *Remove* garlic and excess oil from the pan, leaving only a light layer. *Place* eggplant back in the pan on low heat. *Add* a few spoonfuls of sauce around the eggplant. *Top* each slice of eggplant with 1 tablespoon of fresh ricotta cheese, a spoonful of tomato sauce and a sprinkle of oregano. *Cover* the pan for a few minutes to heat the ricotta, about five minutes. *Remove* cover and *sprinkle* with grated Parmesan cheese. *Serve* with short, curly pasta topped with tomato sauce and more freshly grated cheese. Buon Appetito!

Eggplant Parmigiana
by Tony Melillo

INGREDIENTS

- 1 medium eggplant
- 2 cups all-purpose flour
- ½ teaspoon salt
- ¼ teaspoon pepper
- 3 eggs
- 2 to 3 teaspoons milk

- olive oil (like Bertolli)
- 3 cups tomato sauce (homemade from canned plum tomatoes, or prepared marinara sauce)
- 1 12-ounce package shredded skim milk mozzarella cheese
- grated Parmesan cheese

Preheat oven to 350 degrees. *Peel* the eggplant and slice into ¼-inch thick rounds. In a small paper bag, *mix* the flour, salt and pepper. In a shallow bowl, *beat* the eggs with enough milk to thin them out. *Shake* a few eggplant slices at a time in the flour mixture to coat. *Dip* each slice into the egg mixture and drain in a bowl. *Heat* about ¼ inch of olive oil in a cast-iron skillet and fry the eggplant on both sides in batches until browned. *Drain* on paper towels. *Spread* sauce over the bottom of a 13x9-inch baking pan and *top* with some eggplant. *Spread* with sauce and mozzarella. *Repeat*, making 2-3 layers, ending with mozzarella. *Sprinkle* Parmesan on top. *Cover* with foil and *bake* at 350 degrees for 45 minutes to an hour, until the sauce is bubbly and the cheese is melted.

Farmers' Market Roasted Vegetable Dinner by Marcia Patmos, *Lutz & Patmos*

INGREDIENTS

- Brussels sprouts
- kale, dandelion greens or mustard greens (whatever is in season)
- collard greens
- extra-firm tofu
- aduki beans, white beans or chickpeas
- garlic cloves, crushed
- olive oil
- lemon
- kabocha or butternut squash, skinned and cut into cubes
- vegetable or chicken broth
- sliced ginger
- curry powder
- salt and pepper, to taste
- fresh parsley

Preheat oven to 450 degrees. *Wash*, *de-stem* and *tear* leafy greens into smaller pieces. *Place* greens and Brussels sprouts in a glass baking dish. *Toss* with olive oil. *Add* several whole or crushed garlic cloves to taste and season with salt and pepper. *Bake* at 450 degrees for 20 minutes, stirring occasionally to redistribute oil and keep from burning. *Test* Brussels sprouts with a fork—if it comes out clean, *remove* from oven. If you prefer softer or if you prefer edges of sprouts or greens slightly crunchy/almost charred on edges and veggies slightly caramelized, *cook* 10-20 minutes longer, watching your vegetables closely. *Squeeze* half of a lemon over vegetables. *Place* squash in a glass baking dish or casserole. *Add* vegetable or chicken broth, sliced ginger, curry powder, salt to taste and fresh parsley. *Bake* at 450 degrees for 20 minutes (concurrently with the greens). *Stir* occasionally so it will cook evenly. *Test* with fork after 20 minutes, *cook* to your desired consistency. *Combine* contents of both baking dishes in a large bowl of a nice color that complements the colors of the ingredients. *Serve* with any rice. I prefer a mix of Thai black rice and quinoa cooked in vegetable or chicken broth.

> " There are great farmers' markets all over New York City. This makes dinner and leftovers, depending on how many people you are serving."

Carrot and Seaweed Saute
by Janis Savitt, *Janis by Janis Savitt*

INGREDIENTS
- *1 package hiziki seaweed*
- *1 ½ cups grated carrots*
- *3 tablespoons sesame oil*
- *4-5 cloves garlic, finely chopped*
- *2 tablespoons fresh ginger, finely*
- *2 tablespoons Japanese soy sauce or Bragg Liquid Aminos*
- *whole wheat with flax tortillas*
- *baby arugula*

SPECIAL SAUCE
- *1 ½ cups balsamic vinegar*
- *2 tablespoons maple syrup*
- *1 tablespoon lemon juice*
- *1 tablespoon soy sauce*
- *1 tablespoon umeboshi plum vinegar*
- *3 tablespoons pine nuts*
- *3-4 cloves garlic*
- *4 tablespoons olive oil*
- *2 tablespoons truffle oil*

Soak seaweed in water for 15 minutes to reconstitute. Drain. *Sauté* garlic and ginger together in sesame oil for a couple of minutes. *Add* carrots and sauté until they begin to soften. *Add* seaweed and soy sauce and continue cooking over low to medium heat for 5 minutes. *Scoop* some of the carrot and seaweed sauté onto a warmed flax tortilla, *add* a layer of arugula and *top* with Special Sauce. *Fold* in the sides, *wrap* and eat! Yum! This can also be served cut in half on the angle and served with a side salad of arugula that has been lightly tossed in the Special Sauce. For a vegetarian dinner entree, *serve* with steamed brown rice instead of the tortilla. It makes a lovely presentation and the contrasting tastes and temperatures make a deliciously satisfying meal.

SPECIAL SAUCE
Measure all ingredients into a bowl. *Blend* with an immersion blender. (Everyone should own one of these!)

"In our office, we girls usually dine together for our midday meal. It needs to be quick and easy to prepare, super-nutritious and slimming, of course! I usually make more than needed for one meal, as it can easily be worked into a vegetarian dinner entree later on. I make the special sauce in quantity so I have it ready in the refrigerator. In all, it takes about 15 minutes to prepare lunch from start to finish."

Pommes Toupinel
by Carolina Herrera

INGREDIENTS

- *6 large potatoes*
- *6 poached eggs*
- *1 cup of milk*
- *¼ stick of butter*
- *salt*
- *freshly ground black pepper*
- *thinly grated Parmesan cheese*
- *ground pepper*
- *2 cups of Bechamel sauce*

BECHAMEL SAUCE

- *2 tablespoons of butter*
- *3 tablespoons of flour*
- *2 cups of milk, just at the boil*

Preheat the oven to 350 degrees. *Wash* the skin of each potato well. *Wrap* each potato in aluminum foil and *bake* in the oven for two hours at 350 degrees until flesh can be peeled easily with a knife. While potato is baking, *prepare* béchamel sauce and poach eggs. Once the potato is almost done, *remove* from the oven and *unwrap* foil. *Cut* off the top of the potato ¾ way up. *Scoop* the inside of the potato with a spoon without cracking or damaging the shell. *Prepare* it into mashed potatoes adding: 1 cup of milk, ¼ stick of butter, a pinch of salt, and a small amount of white pepper and mix with finely ground parmesan cheese. *Save* ½ cup of mashed potatoes. *Put* mashed potatoes inside the potato shells, leaving room in the center for the poached egg. *Place* poached egg inside the potato filled with puree, and then season with salt and pepper. *Spoon* a little béchamel sauce over the potato and on top of that, *add* a little more of the mashed potatoes and use a spoon to lift the inside. *Sprinkle* potato with Parmesan cheese, *broil* in the oven for three minutes until the top is brown and crisp. *Remove* from the oven and serve.

BECHAMEL SAUCE

Heat saucepan. *Melt* butter over low heat. *Sprinkle* flour over butter and *stir* with a whisk. *Cook* slowly for about three minutes. Do not let this turn any color. *Lower* heat as much as possible and *add* hot milk little by little.

POACHED EGGS

Boil water in a saucepan until reaching highest boiling point. Eggs are done in batches of two or three in the sauce pan with water boiled, turn heat off. *Place* eggs gently one by one and let there for exactly three minutes under cover. *Take* the eggs out with a slotted spoon.

85

South Philly Cheese Steak
by Kenny Bonavitacola

INGREDIENTS

- *2- 2 ½ pounds eye of round beef, very thinly sliced*
- *2-3 tablespoons olive oil*
- *3 ciabatta or Italian hoagie rolls, split ¾ open gutted and lightly toasted*
      (This is how a bona fide South Philadelphian explains that they want
      more meat than dough in their sandwich!)
- *2-3 slices per sandwich, white American cheese*
- *2-3 slices per sandwich, Provolone cheese*
- *1-2 large Vidalia onions, finely chopped*

NOTE ON THE BEEF: Explain to your butcher that the steak must be frozen for at least 45 minutes prior to slicing in order to insure an almost translucent quality. And if you're feeling adventurous, use Kobe beef.

In a frying pan, *sauté* chopped onions in 1 tablespoon of olive oil until golden brown. *Remove* and place to the side. With the remaining heated oil, *place* several slices of the meat on a griddle, in a grill pan or large frying pan over medium heat. When brown on one side (less than a minute), *flip* and cook the other side. *Stack* the meat in the pan. I prefer to overlap the slices. *Scatter* onions on top of the meat. *Place* white American and Provolone cheese slices on top of meat and onions. *Lower* the heat and cook until cheese is completely melted. The entire process should take no more than 3 minutes. *Use* a spatula to scoop the mixture of meat and cheeses on to the sliced roll. *Add* salt, pepper and condiments to taste.

66 Whenever I make a Philly Cheesesteak the aroma of the fried onions, melting cheeses and toasted roll...transports me to the cherished time I spent as a short-order cook in my grandmother's B&G Luncheonette in South Philadelphia. 99

"Double Your Pleasure" Truffle Mac and Cheese by Cynthia Rowley

INGREDIENTS

- *½ pound of shells or orecchiette pasta*
- *1 ½ tablespoons butter*
- *1 ½ tablespoons flour*
- *1 cup milk*
- *1 egg*

- *1 cup shredded cheese (cheddar, gruyere, or fontina)*
- *Truffle oil or shaved black truffles*
- *prosciutto, cut into 1 inch pieces*
- *Salt and fresh ground pepper to taste*

In large a pot, *boil* the water and cook pasta until al dente. *Drain* and put to back into the pot. While the water is boiling, in a separate pan, *melt* the butter. Once melted, *add* the flour and whisk until thickened. *Stir* in the milk and let simmer for 5-7 minutes. *Temper* and then *add* the egg to the butter, flour, and milk mixture to create a béchamel sauce. *Remove* from stove and pour béchamel over pasta to lightly coat; add cheese and salt and pepper to taste. Stir to coat. *Divide* the pasta into two ramekins. The first ramekin is ready for the broiler. In the second ramekin, *toss* pasta with prosciutto, sprinkling a few pieces on the top. *Drizzle* the mixture with truffle oil or top with shaved truffles to taste. *Place* both ramekins in the broiler. They're ready when they have a golden crust. *Serve* with a salad of fresh greens and warm, crusty bread. To drink, *have* sparkling wine for the adults, and sparkling cider makes a special surprise for the kids. Cheers!

66 A treat for everyone at the table, this macaroni and cheese will please sophisticated grownup palettes as well as picky little ones. 99

Mac N' Cheese
by Jenni Kayne

INGREDIENTS

- 8 tablespoons (1 stick) unsalted butter, plus more for dish
- 6 slices good white bread, crusts removed, torn into ¼-to ½-inch pieces
- 5 ½ cups milk
- ½ cup all-purpose flour
- 2 teaspoons salt
- ¼ teaspoon freshly grated nutmeg
- ¼ teaspoon freshly ground black pepper
- ¼ teaspoon cayenne pepper, or to taste
- 4 ½ cups sharp white cheddar cheese (about 18 ounces), grated
- 2 cups Gruyere cheese (about 8 ounces), grated or 1 ¼ cups Pecorino Romano cheese (about 5 ounces), grated
- 1 pound elbow macaroni

Preheat oven to 375 degrees. *Butter* a 3-quart casserole dish; set aside. *Place* bread in a medium bowl. In a small saucepan over medium heat, *melt* 2 tablespoons butter. *Pour* butter into bowl with bread, and *toss*. *Set* breadcrumbs aside. In a medium saucepan set over medium heat, *heat* milk. *Melt* remaining 6 tablespoons butter in a high-sided skillet over medium heat. When butter bubbles, add flour. *Cook*, whisking, 1 minute. While still whisking, slowly *pour* in hot milk. Continue cooking, whisking constantly, until the mixture bubbles and becomes thick. *Remove* pan from heat. *Stir* in salt, nutmeg, black pepper, cayenne pepper, 3 cups cheddar cheese and 1 ½ cups Gruyere or 1 cup Pecorino Romano; set cheese sauce aside. Fill a large saucepan with water; bring to a boil. *Add* macaroni; cook 2 to 3 minutes less than manufacturer's directions, until the outside of pasta is cooked and the inside is underdone. (Different brands of macaroni cook at different rates; be sure to read the instructions.) *Transfer* macaroni to a colander, *rinse* under cold running water and drain well. *Stir* macaroni into the reserved cheese sauce. *Pour* mixture into prepared dish. *Sprinkle* remaining 1 ½ cups cheddar cheese, ½ cup Gruyere or ¼ cup Pecorino Romano, and breadcrumbs over top. *Bake* at 375 degrees until browned on top, about 30 minutes. *Transfer* dish to a wire rack to cool 5 minutes; *serve* hot.

" This is my favorite macaroni and cheese and was my biggest craving while I was pregnant— I ate it at least once a week. It's the perfect comfort food.**"**

Turkey Chili with White Beans
by John Bartlett

INGREDIENTS

- 1 tablespoon vegetable oil
- 2 medium onions, chopped
- 1 ½ teaspoons dried oregano
- 1 ½ teaspoons ground cumin
- 2 pounds lean ground turkey
- ¼ cup chili powder
- 2 bay leaves
- 1 tablespoon unsweetened cocoa powder

- 1 ½ teaspoons salt
- ¼ teaspoon ground cinnamon
- 1 28-ounce can diced tomatoes
- 3 cups beef broth or stock
- 1 8-ounce can tomato sauce
- 3 15-ounce cans small white beans, rinsed and drained

Heat oil in large, heavy pot over medium heat. *Add* onions and sauté until light brown and tender, about 10 minutes. *Add* oregano and cumin, *stir* 1 minute. *Increase* heat to medium-high and add turkey, stirring until it is no longer pink, breaking it up with back of spoon. *Stir* in chili powder, bay leaves, cocoa powder, salt and cinnamon. *Add* tomatoes with their juices. *Mix* in broth and tomato sauce and bring to a boil. *Reduce* heat and simmer 45 minutes, stirring occasionally. *Add* beans to chili and simmer until flavors blend, about 10 minutes longer. *Discard* bay leaves and serve.

Olive Oil Popcorn
by Norma Kamali

INGREDIENTS

- olive oil
- popping corn
- sea salt

Pour ¼ inch of the best olive oil in the world into a heavy saucepan. My favorite is from the South of France. *Heat* oil until very hot, but not smoking, with the lid on the pot. *Pour* in large kernel popping corn, filling the entire bottom of the pot but not sitting above the olive oil. The best quality popping corn is from Nebraska. *Cover* the pot, and slide it back and forth on the stove until the kernels settle on the bottom and to be sure every kernel is drenched in the olive oil. Once you hear the popping begin, *have* your large bowl ready lined with squiggles of olive oil and sea salt. When the popping slows down quickly *uncover* the pot and pour the popcorn into the bowl. Squiggle olive oil throughout the contents of the bowl and sprinkle sea salt to taste. You will truly enjoy the taste, the scent, and the olive oil on your hands, which you can immediately *use* as a moisturizer.

Meatloaf
by Bill Blass

INGREDIENTS

- 1 cup celery, chopped
- 1 cup onion, chopped
- 2 pounds ground sirloin
- ½ pound ground pork
- ½ pound ground veal (ask butcher to grind meats fresh)
- ½ cup parsley, minced

- 1 ½ cup fresh bread crumbs
- 1 egg, beaten with...
- 1 tablespoon Worcestershire sauce
- pinch of thyme and marjoram
- 1 12-ounce bottle Heinz Chili Sauce
- 5 strips bacon

Preheat oven to 350 degrees. *Saute* celery and onion in butter. In a mixing bowl, *combine* celery and onion with the meats, parsley and bread crumbs. *Add* egg with Worcestershire sauce, seasonings and form loaf. *Top* with chili sauce and bacon. *Bake* at 350 degrees for one hour. *Remove* from the oven and rest—not you, silly—the meat loaf. *Serve* with mashed potatoes, red pepper jelly, corn and lima beans – wow!

Eleanor Banks' Meatloaf
by Jeffrey Banks

INGREDIENTS

- 1 pound ground chuck
- ½ pound pork sausage
- 1 medium small onion, finely chopped
- ½ green pepper, finely chopped
- 2-3 celery stalks, finely chopped

- ¾ cup fine breadcrumbs
- salt and pepper to taste
- celery salt to taste
- 2 small cans tomato sauce
- ¾ pound sliced bacon (optional)

Preheat oven to 350 degrees. *Combine* all ingredients and mix very well with 1 can of tomato sauce. *Shape* loaf in lightly greased or non-stick sprayed Pyrex pan. *Mix* the remaining can of tomato sauce and ½ can of water and set aside. *Place* loaf in preheated oven for ½ hour. After ½ hour *reduce* heat to 325 degrees. *Pour* off excess fat and baste with tomato sauce that was set aside. *Bake* loaf for additional 40 minutes. Internal temperature should be 160 degrees. (*Insert* meat thermometer in thickest part of loaf.) *Remove* loaf from oven. *Tent* with aluminum foil and let rest for 5 minutes before slicing.

Hot Dog Casserole

by Sam Shipley, *Shipley Halmos*

INGREDIENTS

- 2 tablespoons onion, chopped
- 2 tablespoons green pepper, chopped
- 1 tablespoon butter or margarine
- 1 pound hot dogs
- 1 can (15 3/4-ounce) barbecue beans
- 1 can (12-ounce) whole kernel corn
- 1 can (11 1/2-ounce) condensed bean with bacon soup
- 10 refrigerated biscuits
- Prepared mustard
- 1 tablespoon butter or margarine, melted (optional)
- 1 tablespoon toasted sesame seeds (optional)

Preheat oven to 375 degrees. In a 10-inch ovenproof skillet, *cook* onion and green pepper in butter or margarine. *Cut* ten 1-inch pieces of hot dog; set aside. *Thinly* slice remaining hot dogs; *add* to skillet. *Stir* in beans, soup, undrained corn and ¼ cup water. *Heat* and *stir* until it boils. *Roll* each biscuit into a 3-inch circle; *spread* with mustard. *Place* a reserved hot dog in the center. *Wrap* dough around dog; *seal* and make a 1/2-inch slit in the top. *Arrange* biscuits, *seam* down atop the hot bean mixture; *brush* with melted butter and *sprinkle* with sesame seeds. *Bake* at 375 degrees for 18 to 20 minutes. *Dress* with Dijonaise mustard and hot sauce for extra flavor!

“ This is the famous Shipley-Sires Hot Dog Casserole! This is the dish for you when you want something that will fill the belly and you had a burger for lunch. Seriously, I love this so much it's almost my favorite thing to eat. Sounds juvenile but hey, there's no problem with mixing a little youngster stuff in to you life. ”

Psychotic Exploding Chestnut Stuffing
by Gela Nash-Taylor, *Juicy Couture*

INGREDIENTS

- *1 box plain cubed breadcrumbs*
- *1 box herb cubed breadcrumbs*
- *1 cup water*
- *1 handful each of rosemary, thyme, sage and parsley, finely chopped*
- *2 cups mushrooms, diced*
- *2 cups celery, diced*
- *3 medium onions, diced*
- *2 large garlic bulbs, diced*

- *1 large bag chestnuts (3 pounds)*
- *2 organic eggs, beaten*
- *1 bouillon cube*
- *2 cups vegetable or chicken stock*
- *2 sticks Devon Double Cream Butter (If Posh & Becks can indulge in this heavenly butter and still look that good, why can't we?)*
- *Salt (Maldon's Sea Salt, divine)*
- *Pepper*

Grab a massive mixing bowl, *toss* in breadcrumbs and *resist* the urge to nibble them all up. *Warm* water, bouillon cube and vegetable or chicken stock. If time permits, *throw* a dishtowel over your head for a quick facial steam. *Add* the stock and water along with melted butter (it's the holidays so cut yourself some slack when it comes to calorie counting) to the breadcrumbs. *Add* beaten eggs and mix until the crumbs are all moist and gooey, just like a homemade Banana Oatmeal mask. *Sizzle* up those diced onions and garlic in a frying pan and then *add* the diced mushrooms and celery. *Take* a big inhale and start to revel in the deliciousness that is only minutes away. Next up, the seasoning. *Fling* all of those fresh herbs along with the salt and pepper into the mix. Now the most important part of the process. *Slice* an "X" in each chestnut on a cookie sheet and place in the oven at 325° to *broil* until they start lightly popping. This should take about 15–20 minutes which is just enough time to reapply make up, check that BlackBerry and make sure your table setting looks divine. *Take* chestnuts out of the oven, *peel* and give them a semi-fine chop. *Toss* those babies in frying pan with vegetable/seasoning mixture. *Combine* complete mixture with moistened breadcrumbs. Voila! Your stuffing is ready to be placed in the turkey. If cooking stuffing in baking dish sans turkey, *make sure* that each pan is 4 inches deep. *Bake* for 20 minutes until brown at 325 degrees. Remember to be creative by garnishing your bird with chestnuts and parsley aplenty.

**❝ May your Thanksgiving be explosive.
God Bless Julia Child!
God Bless Georgiana the Duchess of Devonshire!
Let Them Eat Couture! ❞**

Big Boy Buttery Popovers
by Jeffrey Costello and Robert Tagliapietra, *Costello Tagliapietra*

INGREDIENTS

- *2 cups all-purpose flour*
- *4 eggs*
- *2 cups milk*
- *1 teaspoon salt*
- *1 stick butter*

Preheat oven to 450 degrees. In a bowl, *beat* the eggs well. *Add* milk, salt and flour and *mix* until fairly smooth (a few lumps are preferred). *Grease* muffin pans with butter. *Pour* in batter, filling each cup ¾ full. *Bake* at 350 degrees for 30 minutes. Please resist opening oven door!! *Take* out when golden brown and puffy. *Butter* generously and serve with your favorite pot roast.

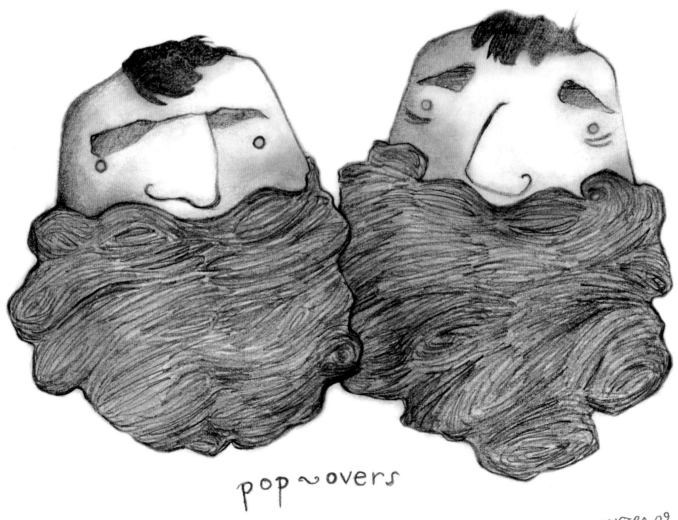

pop ∿overs

RTAGLIAPIETRA 09

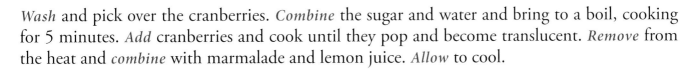

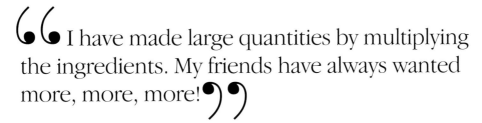

Cranberry Relish
by Joan Vass

INGREDIENTS
- *1 pound cranberries*
- *2 cups granulated sugar*
- *1 cup water*
- *6 tablespoons marmalade (i.e. orange, lemon or lime, or a combination)*
- *juice of 2 lemons*
- *slivered almond for decoration, if preferred*

Wash and pick over the cranberries. *Combine* the sugar and water and bring to a boil, cooking for 5 minutes. *Add* cranberries and cook until they pop and become translucent. *Remove* from the heat and *combine* with marmalade and lemon juice. *Allow* to cool.

> "I have made large quantities by multiplying the ingredients. My friends have always wanted more, more, more!"

German Potato Salad
by Tina Lutz, *Lutz & Patmos*

INGREDIENTS
- *Yukon Gold potatoes, peeled*
- *bouillon cube*
- *yellow onions, diced*
- *mustard*
- *salt*
- *Maggi or Bragg Liquid Aminos*
- *white wine vinegar*
- *sunflower oil*

Make bouillon with the bouillon cube. *Use* a mandolin to slice potatoes into ¼ -inch thick slices. *Place* into the bouillon. *Boil* for 5 minutes, until al dente. *Remove* potatoes, *save* the bouillon. In a separate bowl, *combine* onions, mustard, salt, liquid aminos, lots of white wine vinegar and some bouillon broth. *Pour* dressing over potatoes and let sit for 10 minutes. *Add* sunflower oil and *serve*.

Kay's Kugel
by Kay Unger

INGREDIENTS

- 1 cup whole pecans
- 3 eggs
- ½ teaspoon cinnamon
- 1 teaspoon vanilla extract
- 16-ounce package home style noodles
- 1 stick salted butter
- 1 pound dark brown sugar
- 1 cup sour cream
- ¼ teaspoon white sugar
- 1 cinnamon stick

Preheat oven to 350 degrees. *Add* touch of white sugar and a cinnamon stick to a pot of water. *Boil* water. *Add* noodles and cook till al dente. *Drain* noodles and set aside. *Heat* butter and brown sugar in a saucepan on medium heat. *Butter* and sugar should be melted and just starting to boil. *Pour* mixture into Bundt pan to coat bottom of pan. *Lay* whole pecans on top of the butter/sugar mixture on the bottom of the Bundt pan. *Whisk* eggs, cinnamon, vanilla extract, sour cream, and approximately ¼ teaspoon brown sugar together in a bowl. When sauce has smooth consistency, *add* to noodles. *Toss* noodles until thoroughly coated. *Put* noodle mixture on top of sauce with pecans in a Bundt pan. *Fill* pan with noodles. *Place* in oven and bake at 350 degrees for 1 1/2 hours. *Remove* from oven and let stand. *Cover* Bundt pan with a plate and turn kugel on to plate so pecans will be on top. *Serve* warm or at room temperature.

" Great as a side dish, desert, or breakfast.
Top with a little sour cream or crème fraiche. "

Sweet Potato Casserole
by Carla Westcott

INGREDIENTS

- 3 cups cooked, mashed sweet potatoes
- ½ cup sugar
- 2 eggs, beaten
- ½ cup milk
- ½ cup butter
- 1 teaspoon vanilla extract
- 2 dashes each of cinnamon and nutmeg
- ⅓ cup butter, melted
- 1 cup dark brown sugar
- ½ cup all-purpose flour
- 1 cup chopped pecans

Preheat oven to 350 degrees. *Mix* sweet potatoes with sugar, eggs, milk, butter, vanilla, cinnamon and nutmeg; *pour* into buttered 3-quart baking dish. *Mix* remaining ingredients and *sprinkle* on top of potato mixture. *Bake* at 350 degrees for 25 minutes.

Grandma Deal's "Golden Cream" filled Chocolate Cake by Donald Deal

INGREDIENTS

- *2 cups flour*
- *2 teaspoons baking powder*
- *¼ teaspoon baking soda*
- *½ teaspoon salt*
- *½ cup butter*
- *1 ¼ cup sugar*
- *2 eggs*
- *3 squares dark, unsweetened chocolate*
- *1 cup milk*
- *1 teaspoon vanilla*
- *¼ cup vegetable oil*

FILLING

- *½ cup sugar*
- *3 tablespoons flour*
- *½ teaspoon salt*
- *1 ½ cups milk*
- *2 egg yolks, beaten*
- *1 teaspoon vanilla*

FROSTING

- *4 tablespoons butter, room temperature*
- *¾ cup powdered sugar*
- *1 teaspoon vanilla*
- *3 squares dark, unsweetened chocolate*
- *¼ teaspoon salt*
- *2 egg whites, beaten until stiff*

Preheat oven to 350 degrees. *Melt* chocolate squares together with butter and sugar in a saucepan, *remove* from heat. *Mix* in milk and eggs, add flour, baking powder, baking soda, salt and vanilla. *Add* ¼ cup vegetable oil. *Prepare* three 9-inch round cake pans by greasing them with butter or shortening, then coating them with a layer of flour. *Divide* the cake batter evenly into the three pans. *Bake* 30 minutes at 350 degrees. *Cake* is done if a toothpick can be inserted and removed cleanly. *Remove* from oven and cool cakes on wire racks.

FILLING:

Cook everything but the egg yolks and vanilla for 10 minutes. *Pour* two beaten egg yolks in slowly and cook for two more minutes. *Add* vanilla. Let cool. When cake and filling are both cool, *put* the first layer of cake onto a cake plate and spread filling on top, *add* the middle layer and *repeat* until the three layers are stacked and filled.

FROSTING:

Melt chocolate squares. *Blend* all ingredients except egg whites into melted chocolate. *Fold* the mixture into the stiff egg whites. Be careful not to over mix. *Frost* the sides of the cake, then the top, turning the cake slightly as you frost.

Deep Fried Mars Bars
by Keanan Duffty, *Slinky Vagabond*

INGREDIENTS

- *1 UK or Canadian Mars bar or 1 US Milky Way bar (same thing)*
- *1 cup milk*
- *1 cup flour*
- *1 egg*
- *1 tablespoon oil or fat (use suet for authenticity)*

Chill, but do not freeze, the Mars bar by leaving it in 'fridge, or freezer for a short while. *Mix* the milk, flour and egg in a bowl. *Whisk* together to create a creamy batter. *Heat* the oil. *Coat* the Mars bar completely in batter. *Lower* into hot oil and fry until batter is golden brown. *Serve* while still piping hot. Mmmm … delicious!

> "This is a delicious family recipe. It was handed down to me by my grandmother and has served our family for generations. It's a simple Northern English dish, is easy to prepare and great fun for the whole fashion family. Deep fried Mars Bars can be served as an entrée or a dessert—so versatile. The ingredients in the dish's variations can vary indefinitely, but the procedure will remain more or less the same. For the healthy option, fry the treat in soy oil rather than vegetable oil (it is worth warning of the high saturated fat content this method of cooking produces). This reduces calories and cholesterol."

Virginia Hilfiger's Brownies
by Tommy Hilfiger

INGREDIENTS

- ⅔ cup butter
- 4 squares Baker's unsweetened chocolate
- 4 eggs
- 2 cups sugar
- 1 teaspoon vanilla
- 1 1/4 cup flour
- 1 teaspoon baking powder
- 1/2 teaspoon salt

Preheat oven to 350 F. *Grease* the bottom and sides of a 13 x 9 inch baking dish. In a double boiler, *melt* together: butter and unsweetened chocolate squares. *Combine*: eggs, sugar and vanilla. *Beat* well until thoroughly blended. *Add* chocolate mixture, stir well. *Add* flour, baking powder, and salt and mix together well. *Add* chopped walnuts, stir into batter well. *Pour* batter into prepared dish. *Bake* for 35 to 40 minutes or until a toothpick inserted into center comes out clean. *Cut* in squares after cooling and serve with vanilla ice cream for a delicious and easy to make dessert!

Sweet Mascarpone and Nutella Crepes
by Devi Kroell

INGREDIENTS

- 2 tablespoons unsalted butter
- 2 large eggs
- 1 ¾ cups milk
- 1 ½ cups all-purpose flour
- 1 ½ cups Nutella

- 1 ½ cups mascarpone
- ½ cup water
- 1 tablespoon light brown sugar
- 1 tablespoon vanilla
- 1 tablespoon brandy

Start off by *preparing* batter. In a large bowl, *mix* together the flour, light brown sugar, eggs, water, melted golden butter, and milk until smooth. Once there are no lumps remaining, *add* vanilla and brandy. *Melt* a small dab of butter to prevent the crepe from sticking to the skillet, repeat as necessary. Keeping the stove on medium heat, *remove* the pan from the stove and pour ¼ cup of the crepe mixture into its middle. *Tilt* skillet in all directions so that its bottom is coated in a thin layer of batter. Return skillet to stove for a minute or so. Once the batter begins to bubble, *use* a spatula to *lift* the crepe to check that it is golden around the edge. *Flip* the crepe over and cook until both sides have golden spots, then slide the crepe onto the plate, storing in foil in a slightly heated oven to keep warm. *Repeat* the process until you have used all the batter. *Take* a crepe and lightly *spread* 2 tablespoons of mascarpone and Nutella, carefully mixing the two together with a spoon. *Fold* into quarters and enjoy.

> " Crepes are an easy way to make a delicious versatile dish: whether for breakfast, dessert or served as a snack, crepes are always a good idea. I like my crepes best in the afternoon, for teatime, served for a little 'girlfriends only' get-together. A delicious cup of Earl Grey with just a tiny cloud of milk perfects this afternoon decadence. "

"Adults Only" Chocolate Chip Cookies

by Mark Ecko, *Ecko Unlimited*

INGREDIENTS

- *2 ¼ cups all-purpose flour*
- *1 teaspoon kosher salt*
- *1 teaspoon baking soda*
- *1 egg*
- *2 ounces milk*
- *1 ½ teaspoons vanilla extract*
- *2 ½ sticks unsalted butter, room temperature*

- *1 cup sugar*
- *¼ cup brown sugar*
- *¼ cup caramel sauce*
- *½ shot espresso*
- *1 cup semisweet chocolate chips*
- *1 cup dark chocolate chips*

Preheat oven to 375 degrees. *Sift* together the flour, salt and baking soda in a mixing bowl. *Combine* the egg, milk, and vanilla and *let sit* at room temperature in another bowl. *Cream* the butter in a standing mixer's bowl, starting on low speed. *Add* the sugars and caramel sauce. *Increase* the speed and cream the mixture until light and fluffy. *Beat* it until it's soft like a babies bottom! *Reduce* the speed and add the egg mixture slowly. *Increase* the speed and mix until well combined. *Slowly* add the flour mixture, scraping the sides of the bowl until thoroughly combined. *Stir* in the chocolate chips. *Scoop* cookie dough, with a ice cream scoop (#20 disher to be exact!) onto parchment-lined baking sheets, 6 cookies per sheet. *Bake* at 350 degrees for 13 to 15 minutes. I like to rotate the baking sheet for more even browning every 5 minutes. *Take* out just before golden brown. They will continue to cook out of the oven! This is a major trick to ensuring perfection. *Remove* cookies from baking sheets immediately. Once cooled, *store* in an airtight container with sheets of parchment paper in between.

"We all love chocolate chip cookies. But did you know they have the power to be an aphrodisiac? My variation offers the perfect proportions of white and brown sugar that will ensure the perfect buttery 'SNAP.' The notes of caramel and espresso round out the blend of semi-sweet and dark chocolate chips. Money back guarantee here! Careful when you eat these with a significant other. Serve 'em hot!"

CHOCOLATE

Red Velvet Cake
by Erica Courtney

INGREDIENTS

- ½ cup butter flavored shortening
- 1 ½ cups sugar
- 2 large eggs
- 2 teaspoons cocoa powder
- 2 ounces red food coloring
- 2 ½ cups cake flour, sifted
- ½ teaspoon salt
- 1 cup buttermilk
- 2 ounces water

- 1 teaspoon pure vanilla extract
- 1 teaspoon baking soda
- 1 teaspoon white vinegar

FROSTING

- 8 ounces cream cheese, softened
- 1 stick of unsalted butter, softened
- 1 box powdered sugar
- 1 teaspoon pure vanilla extract

Preheat oven to 350 degrees and *prepare* two 9-inch or three 8-inch cake pans by *greasing* and lightly *flouring*. Using a standing mixer with the paddle attachment, *mix* the shortening and sugar until light and creamy. *Add* eggs one at a time, *mixing* until fully incorporated before *adding* the next egg.In a medium bowl, *combine* the cocoa and red food coloring, making a paste, then add it to shortening, butter and egg mixture. *Beat* until all ingredients are well combined. *Slowly* add ⅓ of the buttermilk, *beat* well, then add ⅓ of the flour and *beat* well, repeat this until all of the buttermilk and flour are mixed in. *Add* the water to the mixture, *beat* well. *Add* vanilla, beat well. *Set* mixer on the slowest setting. *Add* baking soda, salt and vinegar.*Pour* into prepared pans and bake at 350 degrees for about 25 minutes, or until the toothpick comes out clean.

FROSTING

Using a standing mixer with the paddle attachment, *beat* butter and cream cheese until smooth. *Add* the sugar gradually until smooth. *Add* the vanilla and beat until delicious! *Frost* your Drop Dead Gorgeous cake.

Couture Chocolate Cake
by Carey Adina

INGREDIENTS

- ½ cup flour
- 16 eggs, separated
- 2 ½ cups sugar
- 24 tablespoons (3 bars) unsalted, sweet butter
- 16 ounces bittersweet or semi-sweet dark chocolate

FROSTING

- 16 ounces bittersweet or semi-sweet dark chocolate
- 16 ounces heavy cream

Preheat oven to 350 degrees. *Melt* chocolate in a double boiler and *stir* periodically until melted. (If you don't have a double boiler—and I don't—you can create one by filling a pot one-third full with simmering water. *Set* a Pyrex bowl or similar sized, lightweight pot on top for the chocolate.) Meantime, *separate* the eggs and using an electric beater, *whisk* whites until extremely stiff. *Transfer* that gooey chocolate into a large bowl and *mix* in sugar, flour, and lightly beaten egg yolks. *Take* half of the whipped up whites and very slowly fold them into the chocolate mixture, blending thoroughly before adding the balance. *Pour* this batter into two non-stick spring form cake pans (or regular round cake pans that have been lined with waxed paper and buttered thoroughly. *Bake* at 350 degrees for 30 minutes. *Remove* from the oven and cool on a wire rack. This cake will always fail the toothpick test—it is supposed to be oozing a bit in the center, but will firm while cooling. *Chill* it when it's cool.

FROSTING

For the frosting *melt* the blocks of chocolate in the same double boiler pot used for melting the chocolate for the cake. When it's melted, slowly *stir* in the heavy cream. When fully blended, *let* cool and spread mixture between the layers and around the sides, *let* it puddle on top. You can also use whipped cream between the layers and as an additional topping.

NOTE ON EGG WHITES:

The key to stiff egg whites (what is used in meringue) is to be absolutely certain that not a drop of yolk gets into your whites. There is nothing more annoying than cracking and perfectly separation a dozen eggs only to find a bit of yolk falling in with the very last one. It is much simpler to separate eggs if you *take* out two short glasses and empty the white into one and spill the yolk into the other. As you check each one, add it into larger bowls. This recipe rises or falls—literally—on this one step, so *be careful* to check that the whites have not a speck of yellow.

Chocolate Ganache
by Rachel Roy

INGREDIENTS

- *6 ounces bittersweet or semisweet chocolate, chopped into chunks*
- *1/2 cup heavy whipping cream*
- *1 tablespoon pure vanilla*

Heat the cream in a small saucepan. Once it boils, *take* it off the heat. *Add* the chocolate. *Cover* and let alone for 5 to 10 minutes. *Add* extract and/or liqueur and *stir, stir, stir*. It will look as if it will not combine, but it will. A small whisk speeds the process. *Serve* warm if you want to drizzle it or glaze a cake, and *serve* cool if you would like the truffle form.

SPECIAL NOTES:
This recipe can glaze an 8 inch-10 inch cake. The type of chocolate can vary from milk to bitter, and from common to imported, for different qualities. The heavy whipping cream can be skim milk or any butterfat content in between, but use just a bit less liquid as the butterfat goes down. The vanilla can be any pure extract or good liqueur. Goslings Dark Bermuda Rum is great for chocolate, as is Grand Marnier for an orange flavor.

"We use this very versatile and easy, fragrant and very oft repeated recipe in my family. It has only three ingredients, but you can add more for additional flavor. It can be extremely rich or made to be a bit lighter. The type of chocolate can vary. It can be a sauce or coating for ice cream, berries or other fruit, or graham crackers, cookies, etc. It makes a lovely glaze on a cake or brownies. It can be drizzled on plates or desserts while it is warm, or, if cooled, it can be scooped into truffles and rolled in cocoa or chopped nuts, or stuffed with a highly roasted espresso bean or nut. It can be kept in the refrigerator and reheated or snitched in tiny spoonfuls."

Strawberry Shortcake
by Behnaz Sarafpour

INGREDIENTS

- 1 package angel food cake mix
- 2 cups heavy whipping cream
- 2 tablespoons confectioners' sugar
- 2 pints fresh strawberries, sliced

Bake cake according to package directions. *Let* cool. *Slice* cake in half horizontally, making two layers. In a metal bowl *combine* cream and confectioners' sugar; *whip* with electric mixer on medium speed until soft peaks form. *Spread* a thick layer of the cream on bottom layer of cake, followed by a layer of strawberry slices. *Replace* top of cake, pressing gently. *Frost* cake with remaining cream mixture. *Cover* top of cake with remaining strawberries. *Chill* about 15 minutes before serving.

Mrs. Clotilde Zucchelli's Torta de Riso
by Italo Zucchelli, *Calvin Klein*

INGREDIENTS

- ¾ cups of rice
- 6 eggs
- 2 cups milk
- rind of 1 lemon, grated
- 1 small glass Alchermes (an Italian liquor) or Grand Marnier
- ¼ cup sugar
- 3 tablespoons butter

Preheat oven to 250 degrees. *Boil* rice with a pinch of salt for 12 minutes, allowing it to become al dente. *Let* it cool. Separately, *beat* eggs in a bowl with sugar, grated lemon rind, Alchermes and milk. *Add* the cooled rice to the liquid mixture. *Butter* a round cake tin, preferably nonstick, and *pour* in the prepared rice mixture. *Add* pats of butter around the top. *Place* the mixture in the oven at 250 degrees for about 60 minutes. *Remove* from the over, *cool*, *cut* slices and *serve*.

"My mother passed this recipe down to me, but the original recipe has been passed down through my family for many generations. There is something about this dish and the way it tastes and smells that reminds me of my childhood and growing up off the coast of Italy."

Pavlova
by Rebecca Taylor

INGREDIENTS

- 1 ¾ cups super fine sugar
- 6-7 egg whites, room temperature
- 1 teaspoon white vinegar or lemon juice
- 5 teaspoons corn flour
- 2 teaspoons vanilla essence

Place the egg whites and sugar in a stainless steel bowl over double boiler. *Whisk* the whites and sugar together until it reaches a temperature of 100 degrees (it will feel just warm to the touch if you do not have a food thermometer). *Remove* it from the double boiler and *continue* beating it until it is completely cold. When the mixture is cold, *fold* in the sifted corn flour and the vinegar. *Add* the vanilla essence to taste (approximately 2 teaspoons). *Place* a large, deep bottomless cake ring onto a baking sheet lined with parchment paper or a silicon mat, *spoon* in the mixture and level it off with a palette knife. *Run* a knife around the inside of the cake ring to remove it and tidy the edges with a palette knife. Or *spoon* the mixture onto silicon mat or baking sheet lined with parchment paper and shape free form with a warm, wet palette knife. *Cook* in a warm oven (320 degrees) just until the Pavlova starts to crack with little or no color. *Remove* from the oven and allow to cool. *Serve* with whipped cream and fresh fruits.

Cynthia's Apple Crisp
by Cynthia Steffe

INGREDIENTS

- 8 large Granny Smith apples, peeled, cored and sliced
- 2 tablespoons fresh lemon juice
- 1 cup unbleached all-purpose flour
- 1 cup sugar
- 1 ½ teaspoons ground cinnamon
- ½ teaspoon salt
- ½ cup unsalted butter, cold and cut into pieces
- ½ cup coconut
- ½ cup panko breadcrumbs
- ½ cup old-fashioned oats

Preheat oven to 350 degrees. Grease a 9x12-inch baking dish. *Place* a layer of apple slices in the pan and *sprinkle* with some of the lemon juice. *Repeat* the layers until all the apples are in the pan. *Lightly* press down on the apples to even them out. *Mix* the flour, sugar, cinnamon and salt in a food processor fitted with a steel blade. *Add* the butter and process, using repeated pulses, until the mixture resembles coarse meal. *Transfer* to a bowl and toss together with coconut, panko bread crumbs and oats. *Press* the crumb mixture evenly over the apples, making sure the edges are well sealed. *Bake* at 350 degrees until the top is golden brown and the apples are tender, approximately 1 hour. *Serve* warm with ice cream.

Palm Beach Citrus Liqueur Cake
by Lana Marks

INGREDIENTS
- 1 cup chopped pecans
- 1 cup coarsely grated orange zest
- 18.5 ounce package lemon cake mix
- 3.75 ounce package lemon pudding
- 3 eggs
- ½ cup cold water
- 2/3 cup vegetable oil
- ½ cup orange liqueur

GLAZE
- ¼ pound butter
- ⅓ cup water
- 1 cup granulated sugar
- ¼ cup orange liqueur
- zest of one lemon

Preheat oven to 350 degrees. *Grease* a cake pan and sprinkle pecans and grated orange zest at the bottom. *Mix* all the cake ingredients together. *Pour* batter over the orange peel and pecans *Bake* at 350 degrees for 1 hour. *Let* cool, and invert on a serving plate.

GLAZE

Melt the butter in a saucepan, stirring in sugar and water. *Boil* for five minutes while continuously stirring. *Remove* from the stove, and stir in the orange liqueur. *Drizzle* glaze over the top of cake.

Prune Whip
by Geoffrey Beene

INGREDIENTS
- 1 pound prunes
- 1 cup sugar
- 1 cup chopped nuts
- 1 lemon
- 4 egg whites
- whipped cream

Soak the prunes for 1 hour, then *boil* them for 1 hour. *Preheat* over to 300 degrees. *Mash* prunes well and *add* sugar. *Strain* excess liquid, *add* juice from lemon and a small amount of lemon peel. *Put* mixture into a square baking pan. *Beat* the egg whites until stiff and *layer* onto the prune mixture. *Add* nuts. *Place* baking pan in a water bath (a larger pan filled with hot water) and *bake* at 300 degrees for 20 minutes or until top is lightly browned. *Serve* with whipped cream.

Great Grandma Jeannie's Butterscotch Wafers
by Zac Posen

INGREDIENTS

- *1 ¼ cup flour*
- *1 ½ teaspoon baking powder*
- *½ teaspoon salt*
- *½ cup shortening (I use 1 stick of unsalted butter) room temperature*
- *2 cups dark brown sugar*
- *2 eggs*
- *1 ½ cup chopped walnuts*

Preheat oven to 375 degrees. In a bowl, *mix* all ingredients thoroughly. *Turn* dough onto a floured board and *shape* into a roll, or cylinder, about 2 inches in diameter. *Roll* the cylinder in flour and wrap in waxed paper (for those of us in the 21st century, use plastic wrap). *Place* roll in freezer until firm. *Take* frozen roll and slice very thin dough slices. *Place* on unbuttered baking trays not touching. *Bake* for about 12 minutes. *Keep* an eye on them, first they get shiny, then they raise and finally they get golden especially on the edges. *Remove* from tray and *cool*.

❝My great grandmother's recipe for butterscotch wafers has an involved family history. My mom, each of my aunts, and some cousins remember Grandma Jeannie sending boxes of these cookies when they went to summer camp or off to college. Her recipe seems to have been lost until many years later when my mother and an uncle conducted a 'bake-off' to see who could replicate the recipe best. Just recently another generation was ushered into the Grandma Jeannie butterscotch wafer club: at age 3 ½ my nephew, Cyrus Everett Anderson, helped bake his first batch. Needless to say, they evaporated. You might want to double the recipe because they fly!❞

Aunt Elsie's Cherry Sour Cream Pie
by Betsey Johnson

INGREDIENTS

- ¾ cup sugar
- 1 cup sour cream
- 2 tablespoons flour
- ⅛ teaspoon salt
- ½ teaspoon vanilla
- 1 teaspoon cinnamon
- 8 ounces cream cheese
- Pre-baked pie crust
- 2 cups canned sour cherries

Put everything but the crust and cherries in a bowl and *beat* until smooth. *Pour* mixture into the baked pie crust. *Pour* two cups of canned sour cherries on top.

Justin's Sweet Potato Pie
by Sean "Diddy" Combs, *Sean John*

INGREDIENTS

- 2 yellow yams
- ½ pound butter
- 2 tablespoons vanilla extract
- 2 eggs
- 1 tablespoon cinnamon
- 1 teaspoon nutmeg
- ½ teaspoon salt
- 1 cup evaporated milk
- 1 cup sugar
- 1 Pillsbury pie crust

Place yams in a bowl and mash. *Add* butter, vanilla extract, cinnamon, nutmeg and salt. *Stir* until well blended. *Add* eggs, sugar and evaporated milk. *Blend* with an electric mixer. *Pour* mixture into a piecrust and bake at 300 degrees for 40-50 minutes. *Let* pie rest for 20 minutes before serving.

❝I have always loved sweet potato pie. It's one of my favorites. My mother passed this recipe down to me and it is always amazing to have during the holidays.❞

"AUNT ELSIES" Cherry Sour Cream Pie

XOX BETSEY.

1. Put all this in a bowl and beat until smooth:

- 3/4 c. sugar
- 1 c. sour cream
- 2 tbsp. flour
- 1/8 tsp. salt
- 1/2 tsp. vanilla
- 1 tsp. cinnamon
- 8 oz. of cream cheese

2. Pour into baked pie crust

3. Pour 2 cups of canned sour cherries on top.

Brown Bread Ice Cream
by Lela Rose

INGREDIENTS

- *5 tablespoons unsalted butter*
- *1 ¾ cups coarse brown bread crumbs*
- *1/3 cup dark brown sugar*
- *4 large eggs, separated, at room temperature*
- *½ cup superfine sugar*
- *½ teaspoon vanilla extract*

- *1-2 tablespoons rum or brandy*
- *1 ¾ cups heavy cream, very cold*
- *Pinch of salt*
- *1 ½ cups sliced almonds*

In a sauté pan, *melt* butter and then *add* breadcrumbs. *Allow* breadcrumbs to fry, stirring to coat until crumbs begin to crisp, 5 to 10 minutes. *Add* brown sugar. *Cook* until sugar melts and becomes dark and caramelized, 5 to 10 minutes, stirring occasionally. *Remove* from the heat, turn crumbs onto a piece of foil and let cool completely. *Place* the breadcrumb mixture in a plastic bag and crush with a rolling pin, or pulse a few times in a food processor to grind coarsely. *Pulse* almonds in a food processor and spread onto a baking sheet. *Toast* in oven at 350 degrees until golden brown. *Mix* almonds in with breadcrumbs. *Beat* egg yolks together with superfine sugar, vanilla and liqueur (optional), until pale and fluffy. *Whip* cream until soft peaks form (do not over beat). *Fold* whipped cream into the egg mixture. *Using* an electric mixer fitted with the whisk attachment, *beat* the room temperature egg whites together with the salt until stiff but not dry, *fold* into the whipped cream and egg mixture. *Fold* in breadcrumb/almond mixture. *Freeze* for at least 4 hours or until hard. *Serve*. For a regular frozen ice cream, use an "old fashioned" vanilla recipe (one that uses eggs). *Add* ½ teaspoon of almond extract and freeze in an ice cream mixer. Add the breadcrumb/almond mixture

“ “ This is an old Southern recipe and one that my mother has always made. There are two ways to make a brown bread ice cream, as frozen custard and as regular frozen ice cream. I have included directions for both. ” ”

Halo-Halo
by Rafe Totengco, *Rafe New York*

INGREDIENTS
- *1 tablespoon sweet red beans (or sweetened garbanzos or white beans)*
- *1 tablespoon nata de coco (coconut gel, or use nata de pina, pineapple gel)*
- *1 tablespoon kaong (palm seed)*
- *1 tablespoon macapuno (coconut jelly)*
- *1 tablespoon jackfruit in syrup, thinly sliced*
- *2 tablespoons gulaman*
- *2 cups ice cubes*
- *½ cup whole milk, plus additional for drizzling*
- *1 tablespoon haleyang ube (ube jam, optional)*
- *1 scoop of ice cream (suggested flavors: purple yam, macapuno or mango)*

The first five ingredients listed above are sold in jars packed in syrup. You can *vary* amounts, omit, substitute, or add ingredients according to preference. To assemble, *layer* the first six ingredients in a tall parfait glass. In a blender, *pulse* the ice cubes and milk to the consistency of shaved ice. *Scoop* the ice over the layers of sweet ingredients. *Pour* on more fresh milk, *top* with haleyang ube, if using, and a scoop of ice cream, and *serve*. To make a more decadent halo-halo, *sprinkle* some toasted pinipig over the halo-halo and *top* with a small serving of leche flan (custard) along with a scoop of ice cream.

Green Juice
by Donna Karan

INGREDIENTS
- *2 green apples*
- *4 celery stalks*
- *1 cucumber*
- *2 kale leaves or other available greens*
- *¼ white cabbage*
- *½ lemon, peeled*

Pass everything through a juicer. *Blend* with ¼ avocado if desired, for added thickness.

66 Green juice is my thing. I drink it every morning. The antioxidants give me a boost of energy. Chef Jill Pettijohn created this recipe for me. It is very simple—you can add in and substitute other green fruits and vegetables when they come into season. 99

Patsy's Bourbon Slush
by John Truex, *Lambertson Truex*

INGREDIENTS
- *2 3-ounce cans frozen lemonade*
- *1 12-ounce can frozen orange juice*
- *2 cups strong tea (use 4 tea bags)*
- *1 cup of sugar*
- *6 cups bottled water*
- *2 ½ cups your favorite bourbon*
- *ginger ale*
- *mint for garnish*

Mix hot tea and sugar together. *Add* frozen lemonade, orange juice, water and bourbon and mix all together. *Pour* the liquid into a 3-inch baking dish and place in the freezer for 2-3 days, or until mixture is semi frozen. To serve, *scoop* the slush into a short glass, *top* with a splash of ginger ale and *add* a mint sprig for garnish.

Key Lime Mojitos
by Lilly Pulitzer

INGREDIENTS

- 2 ½ cups light rum
- 1 ¼ cups freshly squeezed lime juice (half from key limes if they are available)
- ¾ to 1 cup powdered sugar
- 3 ¾ cups club soda
- 10 large sprigs fresh mint (about 4 to 6 leaves each)
- crushed ice

Stir rum, lime juice and sugar in a large pitcher until sugar is dissolved. *Add* club soda and stir gently. *Divide* mint among 10 glasses. *Using* the back of a spoon, *crush* mint sprigs in glasses. *Add* crushed ice to glasses. *Pour* mojito mixture over mint and ice, dividing equally among glasses. *Drink* immediately.

"Adjust the amount of sugar in this recipe according to your preference. We tend to like it sweet!"

The Natasha
by Sully Bonnelly

INGREDIENTS
- *1 large watermelon*
- *1 bottle of good Champagne*

Cut and *seed* the watermelon, leaving the pink center only. *Scoop* out the pink fruit and *blend* it in food processor. *Place* watermelon juice in a glass and *add* Champagne (1/3 watermelon to 2/3 Champagne). *Enjoy*!

"Inspired in Cuernavaca, Mexico at the home of the renowned collector and heiress, Natasha Gelman, this combination of watermelon juice and Champagne combines the colors of this the 'city of eternal spring' and the vivacity of Natasha. Known for her beauty and charm, Natasha was painted by all of the most important Mexican artists of the 20th century, including her great friends Frida Kahlo and Diego Rivera as well as Rufino Tamayo, whose signature paintings of watermelons hung at the Cuernavaca residence. This is a delight to the palate—a combination of color, freshness and cheer."

The Natasha by Sully Bonnelly
Sketch: Page 122-123

Hot Spiced Herbal Chai
by Cheryl Finnegan, *Virgins Saints and Angels*

INGREDIENTS

- *6 cups water*
- *4 tea bags Roastaroma (by Celestial Seasonings)*
- *2 tea bags Bengal spice (by Celestial Seasonings)*
- *5 generous tablespoons herbal coffee drink (like Teeccino)*
- *2-3 tablespoons vanilla (preferrably without alcohol)*
- *1 tablespoon ginger, sliced*
- *1 cup of whipping cream, whole milk, or soy milk to taste*

Boil all the ingredients, but the dairy. Before serving, *add* the dairy and *reheat.* I love to add a bit of honey to mine.

" This is an original recipe from a dear friend of mine, my mentor and my angel, Jerez Montenegro, from San Miguel de Allende. I love to drink this late at night with some friends or offer it as a decaffeinated option at a dinner party. Everyone loves this drink and they can't believe it doesn't have coffee in it! As an added bonus, your home is filled with this amazing aroma! "

The Questionnaires...

_____'s recipe...

My favorite restaurant: _____

My favorite person to cook for: _____

The ingredient that is most indispensible to me: _____

My favorite "sinful" indulgence: _____

The most sensual meal would include: _____

My favorite cuisine: _____

The most unforgettable meal I have ever experienced: _____

My ideal dinner guest list includes: _____

The strongest memory of my mother's cooking: _____

My idea of a food extravaganza: _____

The most fashionable dish I can prepare: _____

The most edible person: _____

My dream dinner date or location: _____

An ideal dinner party should: _____

The most appropriate time for dinner to begin: _____

My dream pattern or brand of flatware and table settings: _____

_____'s recipe…

My favorite restaurant: _____

My favorite person to cook for: _____

The ingredient that is most indispensible to me: _____

My favorite "sinful" indulgence: _____

The most sensual meal would include: _____

My favorite cuisine: _____

The most unforgettable meal I have ever experienced: _____

My ideal dinner guest list includes: _____

The strongest memory of my mother's cooking: _____

My idea of a food extravaganza: _____

The most fashionable dish I can prepare: _____

The most edible person: _____

My dream dinner date or location: _____

An ideal dinner party should: _____

The most appropriate time for dinner to begin: _____

My dream pattern or brand of flatware and table settings: _____

_____’s recipe....

My favorite restaurant: _____

My favorite person to cook for: _____

The ingredient that is most indispensible to me: _____

My favorite "sinful" indulgence: _____

The most sensual meal would include: _____

My favorite cuisine: _____

The most unforgettable meal I have ever experienced: _____

My ideal dinner guest list includes: _____

The strongest memory of my mother's cooking: _____

My idea of a food extravaganza: _____

The most fashionable dish I can prepare: _____

The most edible person: _____

My dream dinner date or location: _____

An ideal dinner party should: _____

The most appropriate time for dinner to begin: _____

My dream pattern or brand of flatware and table settings: _____

_____'s recipe…

My favorite restaurant: _____

My favorite person to cook for: _____

The ingredient that is most indispensible to me: _____

My favorite "sinful" indulgence: _____

The most sensual meal would include: _____

My favorite cuisine: _____

The most unforgettable meal I have ever experienced: _____

My ideal dinner guest list includes: _____

The strongest memory of my mother's cooking: _____

My idea of a food extravaganza: _____

The most fashionable dish I can prepare: _____

The most edible person: _____

My dream dinner date or location: _____

An ideal dinner party should: _____

The most appropriate time for dinner to begin: _____

My dream pattern or brand of flatware and table settings: _____

_____'s recipe...

My favorite restaurant: _____

My favorite person to cook for: _____

The ingredient that is most indispensible to me: _____

My favorite "sinful" indulgence: _____

The most sensual meal would include: _____

My favorite cuisine: _____

The most unforgettable meal I have ever experienced: _____

My ideal dinner guest list includes: _____

The strongest memory of my mother's cooking: _____

My idea of a food extravaganza: _____

The most fashionable dish I can prepare: _____

The most edible person: _____

My dream dinner date or location: _____

An ideal dinner party should: _____

The most appropriate time for dinner to begin: _____

My dream pattern or brand of flatware and table settings: _____

_____'s recipe...

My favorite restaurant: _____

My favorite person to cook for: _____

The ingredient that is most indispensible to me: _____

My favorite "sinful" indulgence: _____

The most sensual meal would include: _____

My favorite cuisine: _____

The most unforgettable meal I have ever experienced: _____

My ideal dinner guest list includes: _____

The strongest memory of my mother's cooking: _____

My idea of a food extravaganza: _____

The most fashionable dish I can prepare: _____

The most edible person: _____

My dream dinner date or location: _____

An ideal dinner party should: _____

The most appropriate time for dinner to begin: _____

My dream pattern or brand of flatware and table settings: _____

_____'s recipe...

My favorite restaurant: _____

My favorite person to cook for: _____

The ingredient that is most indispensible to me: _____

My favorite "sinful" indulgence: _____

The most sensual meal would include: _____

My favorite cuisine: _____

The most unforgettable meal I have ever experienced: _____

My ideal dinner guest list includes: _____

The strongest memory of my mother's cooking: _____

My idea of a food extravaganza: _____

The most fashionable dish I can prepare: _____

The most edible person: _____

My dream dinner date or location: _____

An ideal dinner party should: _____

The most appropriate time for dinner to begin: _____

My dream pattern or brand of flatware and table settings: _____

_____'s recipe…

My favorite restaurant: _____

My favorite person to cook for: _____

The ingredient that is most indispensible to me: _____

My favorite "sinful" indulgence: _____

The most sensual meal would include: _____

My favorite cuisine: _____

The most unforgettable meal I have ever experienced: _____

My ideal dinner guest list includes: _____

The strongest memory of my mother's cooking: _____

My idea of a food extravaganza: _____

The most fashionable dish I can prepare: _____

The most edible person: _____

My dream dinner date or location: _____

An ideal dinner party should: _____

The most appropriate time for dinner to begin: _____

My dream pattern or brand of flatware and table settings: _____

CFDA Members

1	Joseph Abboud	56	David Chu	110	James Galanos	164	Liz Lange
2	Amsale Aberra	57	Eva Chun	111	Nancy Geist	165	Ralph Lauren
3	Reem Acra	58	Doo-Ri Chung	112	Geri Gerard	166	Eunice Lee
4	Carey Adina	59	Carol Cohen	113	Mossimo Giannulli	167	Judith Leiber
5	Adolfo	60	Meg Cohen	114	Justin Giunta	168	Larry Leight
6	Simon Alcantara	61	Peter Cohen	115	Nicholas Graham	169	Nanette Lepore
7	Linda Allard	62	Anne Cole	116	Cindy Greene	170	Michael Leva
8	Carolina Amato	63	Kenneth Cole	117	Henry Grethel	171	Monique Lhuillier
9	Ron Anderson	64	Liz Collins	118	George Gublo	172	Phillip Lim
10	John Anthony	65	Michael Colovos			173	Adam Lippes
11	Nak Armstrong	66	Nicole Colovos	119	Everett Hall	174	Elizabeth Locke
12	Brian Atwood	67	Sean Combs	120	Jeff Halmos	175	Tina Lutz
13	Max Azria	68	Rachel Comey	121	Douglas Hannant		
14	Yigal Azrouel	69	Maria Cornejo	123	Cathy Hardwick	176	Bob Mackie
		70	Esteban Cortazar	124	John Hardy	177	Jeff Mahshie
15	Mark Badgley	71	Francisco Costa	125	Karen Harman	178	Catherine Malandrino
16	Michael Ball	72	Victor Costa	126	Dean Harris	179	Maurice Malone
17	Jeffrey Banks	73	Jeffrey Costello	127	Johnson Hartig	180	Colette Malouf
18	Leigh Bantivoglio	74	Erica Courtney	128	Sylvia Heisel	181	Isaac Manevitz
19	Jhane Barnes	75	James Coviello	129	Joan Helpern	182	Robert Marc
20	John Bartlett	76	Steven Cox	130	Stan Herman	183	Mary Jane Marcasiano
21	Victoria Bartlett	77	Keren Craig	131	Lazaro Hernandez	184	Lana Marks
22	Dennis Basso	78	Philip Crangi	132	Carolina Herrera	185	Lisa Mayock
23	Michael Bastian			133	Tommy Hilfiger	186	Jessica McClintock
24	Bradley Bayou	79	Sandy Dalal	134	Carole Hochman	187	Jack McCollough
25	Richard Bengtsson	80	Robert Danes	135	Janet Howard	188	Mary McFadden
26	Dianne Benson	81	Erica Davies			189	Mark McNairy
27	Magda Berliner	82	Oscar de la Renta	136	Marc Jacobs	190	David Meister
28	Alexis Bittar	83	Donald Deal	137	Henry Jacobson	191	Andreas Melbostad
29	Sherrie Bloom	84	Louis Dell'Olio	138	Eric Javits, Jr.	192	Gilles Mendel
30	Kenneth Bonavitacola	85	Pamela Dennis	139	Lisa Jenks	193	Gene Meyer
31	Sully Bonnelly	86	Kathryn Dianos	140	Betsey Johnson	194	Carlos Miele
32	Monica Botkier	87	Keanan Duffty	141	Alexander Julian	195	Malia Mills
33	Marc Bouwer	88	Randolph Duke			196	Nicole Miller
34	Bryan Bradley	89	Henry Dunay	142	Gemma Kahng	197	James Mischka
35	Barry Bricken	90	Holly Dunlap	143	Norma Kamali	198	Richard Mishaan
36	Thom Browne	91	Stephen Dweck	144	Donna Karan	199	Isaac Mizrahi
37	Dana Buchman			145	Lance Karesh	200	Paul Morelli
38	Andrew Buckler	92	Marc Ecko	146	Kasper	201	Robert Lee Morris
39	Sophie Buhai	93	Libby Edelman	147	Ken Kaufman	202	Miranda Morrison
40	Tory Burch	94	Sam Edelman	148	Jenni Kayne	203	Rebecca Moses
41	Stephen Burrows	95	Mark Eisen	149	Rod Keenan	204	Kate Mulleavy
		96	Melinda Eng	150	Pat Kerr	205	Laura Mulleavy
42	Anthony Camargo			151	Naeem Khan	206	Sandra Muller
43	Pamela Capone	97	Steve Fabrikant	152	Eugenia Kim	207	Matt Murphy
44	Pierre Carrilero	98	Carlos Falchi	153	Calvin Klein		
45	Liliana Casabal	99	Pina Ferlisi	154	Michael Kors	208	Gela Nash-Taylor
46	Edmundo Castillo	100	Andrew Fezza	155	Fiona Kotur-Marin	209	Josie Natori
47	Salvatore Cesarani	101	Patricia Ficalora	156	Reed Krakoff	210	Charlotte Neuville
48	Richard Chai	102	Cheryl Finnegan	157	Regina Kravitz	211	David Neville
49	Julie Chaiken	103	Eileen Fisher	158	Devi Kroell	212	Rozae Nichols
50	Amy Chan	104	Dana Foley	159	Blake Kuwahara	213	Lars Nilsson
51	Charles Chang-Lima	105	Tom Ford			214	Roland Nivelais
52	Natalie Chanin	106	Istvan Francer	160	Steven Lagos	215	Vanessa Noel
53	Georgina Chapman	107	Isaac Franco	161	Derek Lam	216	Charles Nolan
54	Ron Chereskin	108	R. Scott French	162	Richard Lambertson	217	Maggie Norris
55	Wenlan Chia	109	Carolee Friedlander	163	Adrienne Landau	218	Peter Noviello

219	Sigrid Olsen	250	Alice Roi	282	Maria Snyder	313	Kay Unger
220	Luca Orlandi	251	Lela Rose	283	Mimi So	314	Carmen Marc Valvo
221	Rick Owens	252	Kara Ross	284	Peter Som	315	Koos van den Akker
		253	Christian Roth	285	Kate Spade	316	Nicholas Varney
222	Thakoon Panichgul	254	Cynthia Rowley	286	Gunnar Spaulding	317	John Varvatos
223	Marcia Patmos	255	Rachel Roy	287	Peter Speliopoulos	318	Joan Vass
224	Edward Pavlick	256	Ralph Rucci	288	Michael Spirito	319	Adrienne Vittadini
225	Christina Perrin	257	Kelly Ryan	289	Laurie Stark	320	Diane von Furstenberg
226	James Perse			290	Richard Stark	321	Patricia von Musulin
227	Robin Piccone	258	Gloria Sachs	291	Cynthia Steffe		
228	Mary Ping	259	Jamie Sadock	292	Sue Stemp	322	Marcus Wainwright
229	Linda Platt	260	Selima Salaun	293	Scott Sternberg	323	Tom Walko
230	Tom Platt	261	Angel Sanchez	294	Robert Stock	324	Vera Wang
231	Alexandre Plokhov	262	Behnaz Sarafpour	295	Steven Stolman	325	Cathy Waterman
232	Laura Poretzky	263	Janis Savitt	296	Jay Strongwater	326	Heidi Weisel
233	Zac Posen	264	Arnold Scaasi	297	Jill Stuart	327	Stuart Weitzman
234	Lilly Pulitzer	265	Jordan Schlanger	298	Anna Sui	328	Carla Westcott
235	James Purcell	266	Anna Corinna Sellinger			329	John Whitledge
		267	Ricky Serbin	299	Robert Tagliapietra	330	Edward Wilkerson
236	Jessie Randall	268	Christopher Serluco	300	Elie Tahari	331	Gary Wolkowitz
237	David Rees	269	Ronaldus Shamask	301	Vivienne Tam	332	Angela Wright
238	Tracy Reese	270	George Sharp	302	Rebecca Taylor	333	Sharon Wright
239	William Reid	271	Marcia Sherrill	303	Yeohlee Teng		
240	Robin Renzi	272	Sam Shipley	304	Gordon Thompson	334	Araks Yeramyan
241	Mary Ann Restivo	273	Kari Sigerson	305	Monika Tilley	335	Gerard Yosca
242	Brian Reyes	274	Daniel Silver	306	Zang Toi	336	Jean Yu
243	Kenneth Richard	275	Howard Silver	307	Isabel Toledo	337	David Yurman
244	Judith Ripka	276	Michael Simon	308	Rafe Totengco		
245	Patrick Robinson	277	George Simonton	309	John Truex	338	Gabriella Zanzani
246	Loree Rodkin	278	Paul Sinclaire	310	Trina Turk	339	Katrin Zimmermann
247	David Rodriguez	279	Pamela Skaist-Levy	311	Mish Tworkowski	340	Italo Zucchelli
248	Narciso Rodriguez	280	Amy Smilovic				
249	Jackie Rogers	281	Michelle Smith	312	Patricia Underwood		

The Council of Fashion Designers of America, Inc. (CFDA) is a not-for-profit trade association whose membership consists of 350 of America's foremost fashion and accessory designers. CFDA Foundation, Inc. is a separate, not-for-profit company, which was organized to raise funds for charity and industry activities. Founded in 1962, the CFDA's goals are, "to further the position of fashion design as a recognized branch of American art and culture, to advance its artistic and professional standards, to establish and maintain a code of ethics and practices of mutual benefit in professional, public, and trade relations, and to promote and improve public understanding and appreciation of the fashion arts through leadership in quality and taste.

Acknowledgements

The Council of Fashion Designers of America would like to thank Diane von Furstenberg for her wonderful leadership as its president. She inspires us everyday. This book wouldn't be possible without the contributions of recipes, original sketches and wonderful stories from the many CFDA designers who shared them. To be around such talent is a wonderful thing. The main ingredient of this book is our editor Lisa Marsh. We could not have done it without her. From the beginning she gave 100 percent to this project. We all applaud Lisa for her excellent advice, wonderful writing and endless testing of the recipes. Special thanks to Martha Stewart for our amazing foreword. We are so honored to have her involvement. Nicole Borel-Saladin is much more than an assistant when it comes to our American Fashion books. Her tireless work and impressive organization skills make them possible. In addition, the entire staff of the CFDA—Lisa Smilor, CaSandra Diggs, Karen Peterson, Rachel Shechtman, Katie Campion, Danielle Billinkoff, Amy Walbridge, Sara Maniatty and Keenya Trancoso—are deserving of my thanks many times over. They all work so hard on behalf of the CFDA membership. Thank you to Scott Currie and Stephanie Pate for their outstanding help. We're grateful to Prosper and Martine Assouline, Esther Kremer and Miriam Hiersteiner for being our partners in the American Fashion series.

Steven Kolb, Executive Director, CFDA

This project, which merges my two passions—fashion and cooking, has been most delightful to work on. I would like to thank the CFDA's Steven Kolb and Karen Peterson for letting me share this labor of love. To the many designers who contributed their recipes, artwork and stories, thank you. Nicole Borel-Saladin is most remarkable in her talents for organizing and coordinating the hundreds of components that have gone into this book. Kathleen Ferrall is my go-to girl for seemingly all that I need—research, recipe editing, formatting—and she's brilliant with the little people. Thanks to Esther Kremer and Miriam Hiersteiner at Assouline for bringing this book to life. I cannot possibly express enough gratitude to my partner Dan Mangan and our minis, Lillian Mabel and Daniel Joseph—you make life delicious. Finally, to my mother, Joanne Marsh and father, the late Donald Marsh, who shared many of his kitchen tricks with me, thanks for my love of all things food-related.

Lisa Marsh

Lisa Marsh is a fashion industry veteran. She has worked on staff at Women's Wear Daily, DNR, and The New York Post, and currently is a freelance journalist. Her work has appeared in such publications as People, Elle, Conde Nast Portfolio.com, City, MSN.com and The New York Post. She is the author of The House of Klein: Fashion, Controversy, and a Business Obsession (Wiley, 2003), and Marvin Traub: Like No Other Career (Assouline, 2008). She lives in New York City.